LYNN EVANS

From Valley Boy to Table Mountain

a life in Rugby

TY GWYN

TY GWYN

Published by Ty Gwyn 2021
© Lynn Evans 2021

Lynn Evans has asserted his right under the Copyright, Designs and
Patents Act, 1988, to be identified as the author of this work.

From Valley Boy to Table Mountain

a life in Rugby

TY GWYN

For my wife, Mary

FOREWORD

This is a book urgently in need of being read. The case against the tyranny of excessive structure has been something of a dying voice in the wilderness, especially in the English era of Eddie Jones. Lynn Evans is a disciple of the great French full back, thinker and coach, Pierre Villepreux. Across the Channel in our increasingly isolated Anglo-Saxon rugby world, fewer and fewer understand the essential argument Evans makes.

Lynn was - for his few sins - coach of Oxford University through my three years in that delightful city. He was a delight to work with, talk with and think with. On the evidence of this book, he still is. Anyone with an interest in the game, either in a technical or purely pleasure based sense should read it.

Stuart Barnes
The Times and Sunday Times rugby correspondent

Me and my wife, Mary

ACKNOWLEDGEMENTS

There are so many people who have helped and encouraged me during the considerable length of time I have spent writing this book.

I will begin at the end and mention two quite amazing editors, designers and publishers, in Mike Brain who was responsible for the early editing and designing the book, who is now recovering from a serious illness and Nicholas Hedges, a diligent and relaxed person who has inspired me to continue during some challenging times. Tubby Tyrrell for providing many of the illustrations used and Antonet Valentine who helped edit the photographs.

Ray Palmer, fellow Welshman and school friend who diligently edited my fragile grammar and kept me going with his drole humour. And being the perfect Best Man at my wedding.

Mike Tanner for his encouragement in changing the book material to record my life in rugby and not a coaching manual. Maybe later! Ben Halliday, my first Head Teacher for his counselling and wisdom.

Others who supported include John Batey a lifelong family friend, helpful critic, convert to rugby who shares my philosophy, hopeless at petanque who enjoys a laugh. Also, a host of former players and coaches I worked with, who wrote some generous comments about me and my coaching. Namely Mark Egan, Rupert Vessey, Dai Evans, Andy Williams, John Vaughan, Craig Brown, Mike Tanner, Gary Henderson, Tim Stevens, Ed David, Malcolm Elias and Magnus Eyles.

To Stuart Barnes, who I had the pleasure of coaching (sometimes!) at Oxford University, for his concise and supportive foreword to the book.

To my late brother Alan, an inspiration to me in my youth and beyond. To Eve and Herber, my Mum and Dad, for constantly encouraging me to do the best I could.

There were many coaches who helped me develop my career in rugby, to whom I will always be grateful. There were two coaches who provided me with the motivation to become a coach who acquired greater tactical and technical knowledge about the game. They were Chalky White and Pierre Villepreux who inspired and supported me in their different ways. Great coaches and great men.

My close family provided me with the support and encouragement to keep writing when motivation was low. My wife Mary, a passionate rugby follower, sadly for me of Exeter and England, was a pillar of support. Along with my daughters, Karey and Cressida, and husbands Iain and Cal, with grandsons Cam, Rory and Dougie providing the amusing elements of a quite informal grandfather and grandsons relationship.

Me and my grandson, Rory

CONTENTS

1. My childhood home
2. My intermediate school
3. Risca Rugby club field being prepared for sports day with 100 yard run and mowed track around the edges
4. River Ebbw
5. Cemetery where I worked as a student
6. Pontymister Steelworks belching smoke

4

5

RISCA

My brother Alan and his wife, Jan

INTRODUCTION

As a young boy, growing up in the Western Valley village of Risca, in Monmouthshire, I used to spend my entire school holidays playing games or participating in various adventures.

My street, Gwendoline Road, was a veritable sports stadium. My friends and I played traditional sports, such as rugby, football and cricket and others that we just made up. There was no coaching. We watched sport live, mostly rugby at the local clubs of Risca and Crosskeys. We learned through a combination of our own play and observation of adults playing. Cycle speedway on my grocery delivery bike and the 'Open Golf Event' on the mountain top were innovative competitions.

Pontywaun Grammar school had a limited physical education programme but provided me with good opportunities to play rugby and cricket for the school team. Twenty-a-side touch rugby in the playground, during lunch breaks, honed our evasive running skills, tactical nous and capacity to handle under the severest pressure. I am sure that my friends and I played games for nearly the ten thousand hours supposedly required for elite athletes to practise. We did not have the help of a sympathetic coach, or indeed any coach, to refine and guide us. However, we did develop a great understanding of 'game play' or as it is more readily known, tactical understanding of games. We were able to transfer the skills we learned in one game into other sports and activities. Running from the Newport RFC rugby ground at Rodney Parade to the train station (about two miles), and sidestepping several hundred supporters, engaged me in thirty minutes of intensive, evasion skill work.

Since qualifying as a teacher at St. Luke's College in Exeter, in 1961, I have been coaching rugby and many other sports. In 1964, I attended the first RFU Coaching week held at Lilleshall in Shropshire. Two schoolteachers and coaching pioneers of rugby in England at the time, Ray Williams, who went on to head up coaching in Wales, and Ian Beer, ran this course which had mostly schoolteachers in attendance. This was the first step towards developing a formalised coaching system in the country. When I began as coach for Oxford University Rugby Football Club (OURFC), in 1981, it was not in the capacity as 'team coach'. The wording of the contract, rather quaintly, was 'to assist the captain in the preparation of the team for the University match'.

At that time, I followed the traditional, coach-led method. I organised the session and told the players what to do. Generally, they followed what I told them.

Two events made me question the usefulness of my coaching methods. Firstly, I attended a coaching session, organised by the RFU's Coaching Organiser, Don

Rutherford, which featured Pierre Villepreux, a French rugby coach. What I observed at Marlow that evening made me want to discover more of what looked like the free play I enjoyed in Risca in my youth. This was 'game play' in a relatively unstructured way. The coach was guiding and challenging the players to find solutions to their problems in the games they played.

The second event was the acceptance by the RFU coaching department to develop a 'player-centred' approach to coaching. This placed the players more at the heart of the coaching process and involved them more through the use of questioning. A senior coach with the RFU, Chalky White, had a huge influence on my own development as a player-centred coach. His insistence on attention to detail was legendary. Putting the two processes of game play and player involvement together in the coaching process, seemed to make sense. So, for me, using a game and player-centred approach changed the way I was to coach thereafter.

This book is largely about that process. It is possible to develop free thinking players, able to take more responsibility for their actions in the game. The more traditional style of coaching is far from obsolete. Yet it should be possible to involve the players more in the decision-making process and to let them learn through close interaction with the coach and the game.

What I have found with young players is that they respond to game-play coaching in a very positive way. The coach can challenge them about actions in the game and check whether or not they understand what they are doing. I wish to share this approach with other coaches, in the hope that it is of value in their coaching.

CARWYN JAMES

Following the British Lions tour to New Zealand in 1972, I attended a conference, in London, entitled, 'When the Lions Speak'. The main speakers were the British Lions coach Carwyn James and the captain, John Dawes. Carwyn's contribution influenced my thinking about rugby and how to change our approach to coaching to resemble what was already under way at London Welsh RFC.

Carwyn had observed that New Zealand, despite continuing as one of the world's leading rugby teams, had become robotic in their preparation. For him, the aim was to prepare his team to do the unexpected. He encouraged his intelligent front row forwards, ably led by the astute Irishman, Ray Mclaughlin, to mitigate All Black power, through superior technical and tactical work at scrum and lineout.

He wanted his very gifted threequarters to expand on their individual talents and use their skills to pose constant challenges to the defences. Halfbacks of the calibre of Gareth Edwards and Barry John welcomed the freedom he gave them to choose their options, within the clear strategy he provided for the team. These two gifted footballers possessed an exceptional understanding of the game. Outside them, Carwyn encouraged other talented individuals to make collective contributions that would succeed against a more structured team. The legendary names of JPR Williams, Gerald Davies, Mike Gibson, David Duckham and his influential captain, John Dawes still resonate with today's rugby people.

Very few of the players had previous experience of Carwyn's close attention to detail. The exceptions were members of the Llanelli team, whom he coached. Above all else, he installed in all his players the self-belief necessary to beat New Zealand. He bolstered the mental confidence of the players, by telling them they were

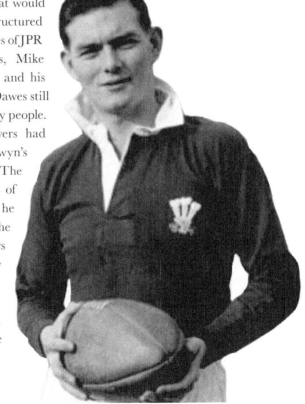

superior to New Zealand. Carwyn believed that players needed to participate closely with the coach in both the physical and mental preparation. It seemed to work rather well on that tour.

In 1973, I was fortunate to see Carwyn coaching the Oxfordshire county team who were preparing for a game in the County Championship. His coaching was purposeful, clear, lucid and engaging for players. It provided a wonderful example to young coaches, of how to get ideas across, by involving the players in the coaching. He was at least twenty years ahead of his time. His death, at far too young an age, robbed rugby of a true coaching genius, who had so much more to give to the game of rugby.

EARLY YEARS

'The purpose of coaching, like teaching, is to exercise the intellect'
Carwyn James late and great coach of Llanelli and the British Lions

June 26th 1938, at Tredegar Cottage Hospital to Eve and Herber Evans, a son Robert Lynn is born. I had arrived in the same hospital as a future Minister of Health, Aneurin Bevan did, many years before. (What a legacy he left in the foundation of the National Health Service).

My parents lived in the Ebbw Vale constituency that Bevan represented in Parliament. They moved shortly before my birth, to the valley village of Risca, about five miles from Newport, in the same Western Valley as Ebbw Vale. My mother was born in Kirtlington near Oxford. She moved to Ebbw Vale when her father became a gardener for the head of the very large steel works, Richard, Thomas and Baldwin, which was the main employer in the town.

More than twenty years later, while playing indoor cricket in Oxford, a local umpire whom I knew from my cricketing pursuits casually asked me if I knew anyone called Isaac. The name Newton came to mind, but after a great deal of thought, I remembered my mother's maiden name was Isaac. He said 'Hello cuz', you are my second cousin! The fact that he gave me out from a dubious run out decision, questioned his family ties with me.

So, I had English roots, a discovery that was quite devastating for a passionate Welshman! My mother was the daughter of the village blacksmith, but somewhere along the line the power genes of the family by-passed me.

My Dad, Herber, was a Welsh speaker, from a Welsh speaking family in Fleur de Lys in the Sirhowy Valley; though he conversed only in English with his family. He was a bus driver with the Western Welsh Bus Company operating out of Crosskeys, the next valley town to Risca. I mention this because, in the late 1940s, my Dad came home one day to tell me he had just driven the bus containing the French national rugby team to their game against Wales at St. Helen's ground in Swansea. I was mortified that he had not taken my autograph book. During the

19

Mum Dad and brother Alan and me in nappy at Barry Island.

second world war he was a member of the Risca Home Guard responsible for protecting the lower steel works at Pontymister, a community attached to Risca.

Our house in Risca was semi-detached with a large lawn at the rear. It was perfect for playing sports. The River Ebbw, full of black water contaminated with washed coal, flowed past the rear of the garden. Literally outside the front door was my school, Danygraig Junior Mixed, which my older brother Alan and I attended. The cul-de-sac road at the front of our house, was not made of tarmac, thus providing an ideal rough surface for the many sports I was to enjoy in my childhood. I imagine that, in the school holidays, my average daily playing time would have been in excess of six hours. Our playground stretched from the river at the rear of our back garden to the tops of the range of mountains of Machen and Twmbarlwm above the valley floor. We were fit, agile and adventurous.

I often reflect on the childhood I experienced both during World War 2 and the post-war period. At that time, education was trying to recover from the loss of so many specialist teachers because of war service. Physical Education lessons were noticeable for their absence. There were so few trained educators. We played games in the freedom of the schoolyard or playing fields.

In this context, a more coach-led approach to games teaching in schools and clubs today tends to restrict this freedom to play. I notice the challenges for young people to balance the time spent on social media and time available for 'free play'.

Thinking about rugby, how can the coach of today release some of the control in coaching to allow players more opportunities to find their own solutions? It is apparent that the more effective learning takes place when the learner has more ownership of the learning environment.

Risca was situated in a wide valley. Two rivers, the Sirhowy and Ebbw had converged near Crosskeys and our community stretched up the side of the valley. There were communities within communities. My area contained a number of semi-detached houses and residents with a relatively higher income bracket, though not middle class. Our tightly-knit communities tended to stay together. In sport we organised impromptu football matches against each other. One such community, housing many who worked in heavy industries such as coal and steel, called Hill Street, often challenged us to a game of football. They were the 'street fighters' of Risca. Their ground, on the side of a hill with a gradient of at least one in three, presented us, the 'bottom of the valley boys' with a real tactical problem. How could we manage to score going uphill? We didn't solve the problem and duly lost. It was through confronting such issues that we started to find better solutions. We alone had to find the answers. There were street gangs of boys who frequently challenged other streets to battle with stone fights. Our street group had to counter the more aggressive gangs with clever forms of tactical retreat. There was no coach!

Half an hour before school started, I would squeeze between a hole in the fence to partake in the many-a-side game of football that preceded the school day. The age range was eleven to fourteen years. The only ball available was a white tennis ball. I still treasure the goal I once scored to win the game just as the morning handbell to start school rang out. The ball bounced up towards my right shoulder, and with my back to goal, (two elm trees conveniently situated about a goal-width apart), I swivelled and hit a glorious shot just inside the far elm. I could then chant the daily, teacher-led maths tables with a smile on my face.

What skills and challenges these conditions provided. We were free to play without any adult supervision. The older players, more experienced, stronger and skilled, provided us 'young ones' with the big challenge to compete in the game. Through observing and playing with the senior boys I think we enhanced our tactical and technical skills.

I vividly remember some of the games we played between the ages of six and twelve. These were very formative years available for skills training. We enjoyed the seasonal games of conkers and ice-sliding in the schoolyard. The game of jackstones, in which you juggled five star-shaped metal pieces into a variety of pick-ups and throws in your hands, helped to develop hand and eye co-ordination. We improved a range of our skills through a team game we invented using three sticks

Aged 7 at Danygraig Infants School Risca fourth from left top row (angelic!).

placed against a wall. This began by throwing a tennis ball from around ten metres to dislodge the football shaped goal and try to rebuild the sticks. The other side could eliminate you by throwing the tennis ball to hit you. There were few gentle throws, as you tried to rebuild the goal. Health and safety were not important issues in those days! Both teams wrestled to find the most effective tactics. Why do we not ask rugby players to come up with their own ideas to invent games? These games could be simple, against themselves, where they try to increase their own scores with a skill or make the game more challenging. Playing could involve sessions of one versus one, two versus two and small-sided games.

Cricket was a favourite game of mine. When I was around eight years old, I had my first cricket bat. Once when I was practising outside my house, my brother Alan came over to me and told me I was batting the wrong way around! I was batting left- handed. He made me bat the other way around which was uncomfortable for me. I often wonder if his action hindered my career to be a first-class cricketer! I was and still am a naturally left-footed player.

Our back lawn was the venue for international rugby games with my friends in winter. In the summer it served as the ground for Glamorgan's county cricket team versus any other team. The rules of cricket included 'six and out' if hitting into next door's chicken run, as the grumpy owner rarely allowed us to have our ball back. We experimented with our batting and bowling. We worked out variations of pace and spin bowling, as well as innovative batting techniques. I would spend whole days watching Glamorgan's cricket team play in the County Championship. In the immediate post-war days Glamorgan played their matches all over Wales, from Abergavenny in the east to Llanelli in the west. I always took along my haversack containing lunch, and my bottle of Tizer. The Tizer bottle was the vital cricket bat, used in our made-up game at the lunch and tea intervals in the outfield. The tennis ball was again the ball of choice, no other sort available. Here we would try and emulate our heroes in the Glamorgan team. They included the classy batsman Gilbert Parkhouse, the medium-paced left-arm bowler, solid batsman and agile close fielder Allan Watkins, and off-spin bowler Don Shepherd. We could hit the ball anywhere on the outfield. The playing square was naturally out of bounds. Glamorgan's redoubtable captain was Wilf Wooller. He was a double Cambridge Blue at rugby and cricket. Wooller would lead his team out when fielding. The warm up was more connected to rugby than cricket. This was not surprising as more than half the team played top class rugby in winter. They were an outstanding fielding side when winning their first county championship title in 1948. Their athleticism, I believe, owed much to their all-round agility and speed connected with their rugby playing. Such was my passion for watching Glamorgan and top-class cricket that I was once fortunate to travel back on the train from Cardiff with the South African touring team. They had been playing Glamorgan on their tour to the U.K. John Arlott the celebrated BBC commentator was in their carriage and invited me and my friends inside to get their autographs. Speaking with these Test players was a huge thrill.

Seeing live rugby matches at the highest level influenced my love and knowledge of the game. I attended my first rugby international at the former Welsh National Stadium, Cardiff Arms Park. In those days the Welsh rugby team was selected by five committee men, known as the Big Five. One of the Big Five just happened to live in the next street to ours. No problem getting a treasured standing only ticket. The match was Wales v Ireland. My brother took me as I was only twelve years old. We arrived four hours before kick-off and secured our place on the perimeter fence on the half-way line. For me the stand-out memory was the fly-half duel. For Ireland, the veteran fly-half Jackie Kyle was an elegant distributor of the ball and possessed a keen tactical awareness. The debutant for Wales was the will-o-the wisp Cliff Morgan. He was a darting, busy and exciting runner. That day saw the birth of a new Welsh star. A star that went on to enjoy a long career in sports' broadcasting with the BBC. Cliff's other major role, when touring with the Lions, was to lead the choral singing for the team. Cliff and I then have something in common, as I will describe later in the book, with the conducting of many a choral session in many lands.

I must be among a diminishing number of Welshmen to witness Wales beating the All Blacks. Thanks to Mr. Harris, the Risca man of the 'Big Five', my brother and I had tickets for the epic game in Cardiff in 1953. The Welsh wing forward, R.C.C. Thomas, cross-kicked from the wing for Ken Jones the Welsh sprinter to gather the ball in the centre of the field and race over for the winning score. Happy days!

Gwendoline Road was in effect a multi-purpose stadium. One day it would serve as Somerton Park, home of Newport County's football team. The next day it would be a home for rugby as Cardiff Arms Park where Cardiff RFC and Wales played. On occasions it was a speedway track. Wales had a speedway team near Bridgend, between Newport and Cardiff. Speedway races on our grocery delivery bikes were lethal and very competitive affairs. The only times I returned to the house during holiday times was to replenish my supplies of energy. Along with my friends, we invented many games. We adapted the rules to ensure fair competition. These rules applied to team selection so that we ended up with as balanced teams as possible. Rules tried to avoid possible safety issues. We made restrictions according to geographical problems, neighbours' gardens or windows. To protect small players against very big ones the rules included 'Big boy cannot tackle small boy'!

In the school yard we played games and pastimes that were current at the time, ranging from marbles and tag games to cigarette card swapping! These games had one thing in common, they were always very competitive, often resulting in arguments. The mountain close to our house was called The Graig. It was on undulating ground near the summit, that we designed our 'Open Championship' putting course. The mountain grass was close cropped and perfect for putting. Holing out with a rusty putter, on a hole half way up a one-in-three slope, was rather difficult. We would stay on the mountain for hours at a time. It took us over half an hour to get to the venue. How fit we were then! There was a Welsh Ryder Cup player called Dai Rees. I usually got his name first in any competition. When I play golf today, my approach shots to the putting greens on the golf course are very inconsistent yet my putting is pretty decent.

At the top of our road was a small shop selling general stores. It was known as Davies the Bread. The owners had three sons who were then all in their 20s and 30s. The eldest, Dai Davies, was an outstanding all-round sportsman. He played football for the village team in a Welsh regional league. He was also a fine cricketer. Dai, a wicketkeeper/batsman played for Pontymister, the next village down from Risca, in the highest Welsh league cricket. He also played regularly for the Glamorgan County second XI. One morning, after working on a night shift at the local steelworks, Dai as normal, went to his bed to catch up on his sleep. He never made it to the bed! A group of local boys including myself, went past his house kicking a football around and generally being rather noisy. A voice called down from Dai's open window, 'Any room for another player'. We were only too delighted that Dai would join us for our kick-about. He left the house before his mother could stop him! Dai was a boyhood hero of mine. He encouraged us young lads with coaching tips. The coaching was generally informal and done during the process of the game. Dai could kick a rugby ball a long distance. Outside his house we often played a game of 'kick gains'. A game in which you tried to kick the ball to cross an end line. The pitch was over a hundred yards in length. If you caught the opponent's kick you could take five forward strides before kicking. Sometimes we would 'grubber kick' the ball along the ground to stop a clean catch. Of course, you sacrificed distance with this method. Dai was in fact our casual coach.

At the bottom of our road was the Risca Rugby Club ground. This was a typical valley team. It played at the second level of Welsh rugby, below the likes of Newport, Swansea and Crosskeys, but still a good standard of rugby. Our young group would watch the first team play every home game. One of our important roles was to man the pulley system across the river that collected balls kicked into the river from the game. This system of collecting balls had its problems, especially when the river was in full flow after heavy rain. If the ball landed in the river close to the pulley, there was no time to save it before it passed the pulley. Next stop for the ball was the Bristol Channel near Newport at the mouth of the river.

We learned about positional play and the different ways of playing a fifteen-a-side game. We had our local heroes. I remember particularly the full back Terry Jones. He had both knees wrapped in bandages, was an elegant punter of the ball and an immaculate tackler. I would try to copy him! As my best friend, Brian Purnell, lived on the boundary of the rugby club, we had easy access to the ground. Impromptu games in the dead-ball area were common. However, we had to be quick to climb back over the wall if a Risca committee man appeared at the bottom gate. Our games in the dead-ball area posed great tactical challenges.

Our local café in Risca was owned by a lovely Italian family called Segadelli. One of their sons Romeo, a good friend, often played in these games. He weighed over fifteen stones and was rather overweight. He could rarely catch us but if a player was held with the ball Romeo would arrive and pull the ball carrier to the floor and sit on him. One such experience was enough for me.

I was beginning to attend more first-class games played at Crosskeys and Newport. They were quite easy to access and not too costly, as I had a free bus pass. Watching the many gifted players in Wales was an education for me. Bleddyn

Williams, a legendary Welsh centre playing for Cardiff, would frequently sidestep his way through a randomly organised set of forwards, with superb balance and elegance. Roy Burnett, Newport fly-half, and one of many Welsh fly halves endowed with skill, vision and pace, excelled when playing against the tightest of defences. In general terms, the West Walians, notably from Llanelli, tended to produce the more ambitious back play, while the hardened men from the Gwent Valleys, from coal mines and steel works, dominated forward play.

The list of gifted Welsh No.10s is endless, including the likes of Carwyn James, Barry John, Phil Bennett, Jonathan Davies and Stephen Jones. The present team of Llanelli (The Scarlets) have the reputation, one might say a duty, of producing rugby of an ambitious nature, to identify with the culture of the town. Culture has a massive influence on how rugby is played, even in a rugby world seemingly copying what people conceive as winning rugby. French rugby 'flair' is not a result of the influence of warm weather but a way of playing demanded by certain regions of the country. Beziers on the south coast of France play rugby more associated with the steamroller forwards of Pontypool in their heyday. Forwards in those days had no need for the artificial strengthening programmes required of modern players. Their hard-manual jobs saw to that. The natural lifting, carrying, cutting work they performed, using efficient and repetitive movements, suited well the demands of rugby. The backs often had less physically taxing jobs. Perhaps teachers, clerks and doctors were the thinkers, but as a former teacher, I could be on dangerous ground with that remark!

Looking back, I realise that this period was perhaps the start of my rugby education for both playing and coaching. I was absorbing so much through observing these very talented players and trying to copy their tactical and technical skills. These were players who excited me. We youngsters wanted to copy their skills. They were our heroes.

The nearest first-class club for me to watch was Crosskeys, just a few miles up the valley from my home. The ground Pandy Park, like many valley clubs, had the river along one side of the field and mountain on the other side. This mountain provided a natural viewing area for watching the games. Crosskeys, a relatively small club compared with the giants of Newport, Swansea and Cardiff, could still cause major upsets on their home ground. Their forwards had a reputation for their very physical approach to the game. Not many teams fancied the Keys on a wet day at Pandy. I returned on several Easter Tours to play against them for Oxford RFC. We never beat them!

The Barbarians toured Wales every Easter, playing games against Penarth, Cardiff, Swansea and Newport. The Barbarians fielded players mostly from the other home nations. Of course, the tradition was to play open and adventurous rugby. I never missed the Easter Tuesday game at Newport. One year a French wing called Pomathios played at Newport. There was this six-foot plus winger, tanned, with very short shorts, who stood out with his speed and agility. I thought he came from another planet. The excitement of watching the Barbarians play was special. Their strategy was first to entertain with the ball in hand. What a joy for us every Easter to see this multi-international group of players play with such freedom.

PONTYWAUN GRAMMAR SCHOOL RISCA

Moving to the local grammar school in 1949 I took my first steps in playing organised sport. I should clarify sport to mean rugby and cricket. These were the only team games provided in most schools at this time. There was not a coach in sight, only teacher supervisors. We did have a PE mistress who taught gymnastics, but only in Years one and two. One young teacher, Johnny Herbert had recently joined the staff. He was an enthusiastic supporter of rugby and took over the management of the first team. He was not a coach but offered snippets of advice and supervised us in our matches. A few local players came to the school on an ad hoc basis. They offered some tips on techniques and, occasionally, tactical advice. Pontywaun provided many players to the local first and second-class teams at this time. Two especially gifted players went on to play for Wales. Jacky Hurrell played for Crosskeys and Brian Jones for Newport. Both were centre threequarters. The schools were the providers of young talent for the clubs as no mini-rugby existed in the clubs. You could play club rugby only after the age of sixteen. To gain selection for the Welsh Schools' team entailed selection for your county team and then further nomination for the very competitive National Trials between East and West Wales Selection XVs.

Though there was a minimal Physical Education programme at the school, we did have an annual House cross country race that meandered through Risca and the neighbouring Pontymister. It proceeded up the side of the valley along the Risca canal that exited into the river Usk in Newport.

I was in the first year at Pontywaun School in 1949 and the race was run on a staggered handicap system, with the youngest going first. I was in the lead group. I discovered quite soon that I could keep going at a decent speed and not slow very much. There were some senior boys who were strong runners. I kept going, not certain where I was in the field. Not many seemed to pass me, except a senior pupil, one Titter Tompkins, who virtually flew past me. On arrival at the finish I learned that I was in second place. My joy knew no bounds. From a rugby point of view, I knew I would have stamina, but the fast twitch muscle required by the speedsters was deficient. I knew even at that stage of my life I would have to become ultra-skilful and develop more cunning and wit in my rugby.

My brother Alan, an open side wing forward, went on to captain the first XV. He was a renowned tackler. Alan had a shrewd rugby brain and was a thoughtful leader. (He later forged a career in the Royal Air Force as a navigator). He had many battles with the talented number 10s representing the grammar schools in Monmouthshire. Ianto James, a fly-half from Abertillery Grammar School, went

My friends in Risca up Machen mountain for a teenage picnic.

on to have trials for the senior Welsh team. He is the grandfather of the Olympic cyclist Becky James, wife of current Welsh player George North. Sometimes it is in the genes. Why did Wales produce so many gifted number 10s, the so-called outside half factory? Observing gifted players going through their repertoire of skills and inventive tactical choices is surely a sound blueprint for a young player to copy. That is how I learnt those devious Welsh ploys. One school friend of mine, Ray Palmer, an amazing man, studied Greek, Latin and Roman History at A level with the same teacher, who happened to be Johnny Herbert. Ray played rugby for the school team and continued to be involved in my future life from time to time, being best man at my wedding and then playing for Oxford RFC with me in the mid-sixties, before embarking on a career in education around the UK. We have recently met up again and renewed our friendship.

The games for the school first XV were against grammar schools of similar size situated mainly in the Western Ebbw Vale Valley. We played our home games on the Stores Field, home of Risca RFC. My most memorable game was also my first. We played the mighty Pengam Grammar School, home to many Welsh Schools Internationals, including future British Lions captain John Dawes. Early in the season, Pengam had beaten Pontywaun in Pengam by over 30 points. At Risca, with a 'home' referee we were a different proposition. My brother was captain for this game and his fellow players encouraged him to select me because they thought I was a decent tackler. The team played heroically in defence and with a few generous officiating decisions achieved a remarkable 3 – 0 penalty goal victory. Pengam refused further fixtures against us!

A number of the school team also played for Risca Youth (u18) team. This meant we played school rugby on the Saturday morning followed by another tough game in the afternoon. As a result, we felt absolutely exhausted! In the evening, members of the team went to the local Saturday night cinema. Most of us fell asleep within a short time of the film starting. These were active days.

During the 1950s Risca became the centre of almost the whole of the Western Valley. A Sunday in Wales in this period was heavily influenced by the church. A large percentage of the population attended church or chapel on Sunday. No shops were open apart from the two Italian cafés. How did the Italian Catholics manage that? My brother and I attended Sunday School until we were eighteen. Our Sunday School teacher was a six foot plus giant of a man, named Ivor Roberts, quietly spoken and a former second row forward of the Risca RFC. Our teenage group agreed we would discuss his bible text on the promise of fifteen minutes to discuss the weekend's rugby events. He seemed to like this treaty as he got completely immersed in it. Under the pretext of a Sunday walk we would manage

In pensive mood age around 15 up Twmbarlwm mountain near Risca.

a crafty game of cricket or football in the small village of Ochrwyth, two miles up on the mountain side. Another chance to practise on a one-in-three gradient hillside pitch. A special activity on Sunday in Risca was the so-called 'Monkey Parade'. Teenagers from far and wide descended on Risca High Street to walk up and down from the Palace Cinema to the Italian Café, a distance of around half a mile. Groups of boys and groups of girls going through the rituals of eyeing up each other. Mostly our group of boys would share banter about rugby with our rivals from other villages in the valley. I was more interested in the rugby banter! This ritual continued for several hours before home-time beckoned. Even today there is an annual get together of former pupils of Pontywaun Grammar School in Cwmbran near Newport. Sadly, each year the numbers are fewer.

Our preparation for matches included twenty-a-side games of touch rugby on the hard-court tennis area during break-times at school. These provided excellent opportunities to hone evasive running skills in such limited spaces. You had to find solutions to the difficult problems of beating defenders and passing accurately.

One memory, forever imprinted in my mind, occurred in a Youth game against New Tredegar. Playing against Risca that day was a young prop forward of gargantuan proportions. He could also run a bit. His name was Denzil Williams, who went on to represent Wales and the British Lions on many occasions. I was playing full back, and as he broke clear from a lineout, he headed straight for me. My options were limited, tackle or move out of the way. As a former boy scout, I had to rule out cowardice. I stood my ground. Then, as I slowly recovered, I heard the calls 'great tackle Lynn'. A tackle it was not. It was a collision between unequal forces. As the stars in my head cleared, I thought I have to learn to position myself in areas well away from players like Denzil! I made my debut for the Risca RFC first XV in my last year at school. The game was against Blaina, a formidable village team from the head of the valley. It was a tough baptism and more physical than I expected. I played in the centre as I was too small for senior rugby as a forward. I was late-tackled early on. Our captain, a former first-class player from Ebbw Vale, picked me off the ground and whispered in my ear, 'Don't worry I know who dunnit'. Minutes later, after a lineout, I saw the late tackler prostrate on the floor. I imagine this was the result of our captain's short hand jab to his jaw. Those were the days of summary justice.

Every Christmas morning, Risca and Crosskeys played a local derby game at second team level. My first experience of this very competitive festive game was in my last year at school. The spirit of joy and goodwill to all men was noticeably absent. I treated the ball like a hot potato as I wished to be in one piece to enjoy my mother's Christmas lunch. Welcome Lynn to the reality of Welsh club rugby.

These experiences were to prove valuable for my survival in the senior game. I think we won that game with a penalty goal. This meant Christmas cheer all round.

I went on to play at blind-side flanker as generally I enjoyed the contact aspect of rugby. I became vice-captain of the first XV. I also was elected captain of the school first XI cricket team. I enjoyed the summers playing cricket for the school in the mornings and for Crosskeys adult second team in the afternoon. The second team captain Byron Denning, went on to become official scorer for Glamorgan County Cricket Club for many years. Here was an opportunity to learn, from adult cricketers, the finer points of the game as well as to enjoy the odd illicit pint of beer after games. As a result of my excessive involvement in sport and my reluctance to study and revise for A level exams, I failed to pass any of my three subjects. As I had already been accepted for a teaching course at St. Luke's College in Exeter, I knew where my future career was heading.

There were two years to wait before entering college. Military service was awaiting. Within a month of leaving school I had received my National Service call up papers. The next part of my life was to serve in the Royal Air Force for two years.

NATIONAL SERVICE

'With 'Teaching Games for Understanding' players can learn about the game and practise skills and techniques within the concepts of a game rather than separate from it. Learning in context provides a sound understanding of the game and opportunities to apply skill and technique under pressure.'
Lynn Kidman 2005 Lecturer and Author Teaching Games for Understanding

I left Pontywaun Grammar School at the end of my sixth form studies. In 1956, I was working temporarily for the local council as an assistant grave digger and grass cutter. I learned little about rugby skills in this job. However, extending tea breaks, hiding behind gravestones when needing a rest, and learning how to play gin rummy from the head gravedigger, were all valuable life experiences. Lining up with all the council workers every Friday for payday, made me feel very grown up. My working life was to be cut short. My call-up papers arrived in late July informing me that I would spend my next two years doing compulsory National Service, serving my country in the Royal Air Force. In early August, I was to leave my home and Wales to live in countries I never knew existed.

After a week's initiation at RAF Cardington near Bedford, I had a posting to RAF Hednesford, a base near Stafford. Here was a schoolboy making the transition to manhood in double quick time. The training was tough and challenging. The physical training, the daily drilling of marching and doing rifle drills as a large group appealed to me. The team ethics were evident. The drill instructors imposed a strict discipline occasionally allied to delivering some most amusing

National Service square bashing group at RAF Hednesford fourth from the left top row

one-liners. One morning as we were in full marching mode, one guy let out a long and sustained fart. Without breaking step, the D.I. shouted 'Fall out the man playing the Trumpet Voluntary'. I just broke up with laughter but maintained my marching rhythm. My prowess with the 303 Rifle and Bren gun on the station's shooting range was not of a high order. The rumour was that expert shooters went to the front line of military action. The Suez crisis had just started. I ensured that I just passed the target test. I also made sure that one of my rounds with the rifle missed the target completely, ensuring a role far from the front line. Not only did we do drill, we engaged in a gymnastics programme and cross country running. Accordingly, we developed high levels of endurance and strength. These served as excellent conditioning for the start of the rugby season. The services have always been enthusiastic to promote sport. The benefits of mixing with the ranks from officers, NCOs and new recruits on equal terms were apparent on the rugby field.

During my first week, a note appeared on my bed in the barracks telling me

Football team of RAF Sharjah in Trucial States second left top row

to attend the gymnasium for rugby selection trials. The RAF had records from our schools and knew what sports we played. What I did not expect was a group of recruits and permanent staff at the base who were already playing top class rugby. Though I was only there for eight weeks, I played for the station's team most Wednesdays. Our training sessions were mostly about team organisation and some fitness work in the gymnasium. What impressed me most was the confidence of the players who had played first class rugby and how they encouraged the less experienced players. Also, playing with these players, somehow raised your own expectations of your game because you did not want to let them down. Training for rugby was a much better proposition than slaving away laboriously on RAF duties. Playing on the wing, a position with which I was unfamiliar, presented me with the challenges of positioning, defence duties and general familiarity of where I should be at any particular time. These issues made me more aware of the differences of positions on the field when the game was in movement. The fitness levels of the threequarters, in the areas of strength, speed and agility were considerably higher than mine. Then, we had to move on to what they called trade training. I could not choose and was told I would be training to be a typist. At the time, only women did these occupations! Typing I did, and, to my surprise, managed to develop a typing speed of fifty words a minute. Little did we know that the computer age would elevate this skill to new levels.

The trade training depot was at Credenhill near Hereford. The base for the elite SAS was close by, so I was pleased not to mistake which depot to attend. I began to realise how important it was to play sport in the services. I managed to gain selection for the station's team on the wing. The back division consisted of one of the most talented back divisions I ever had the pleasure of playing in. The scrum half had played professional rugby league. Our number 10 was Ken Richards of Bridgend and Wales, at 12 was Brian Richards of London Welsh and Wales, at 13 Mike Wade of Cambridge University and England, at 15 Ray Cheney of Pontypool and Newport, and I of Pontywaun Grammar School and Risca. We won all our games in the three months I played, mostly scoring in excess of forty points a game. People talk about steep learning curves and this one was precipitous. I had moved up so many levels of playing. The game became so much easier for me as my fellow threequarters made so much time and space for me on the wing. As a result, despite a lack of real speed, I scored in nearly every game. I was beginning to pick up how these players were reading the game and how their individual skills were consistently accurate and precise. Playing alongside skilled performers gave me more insight on why they were playing at this level. They nearly always seemed to have more time to execute skills under pressure than less experienced players. This experience of watching and playing with skilled performers, was to influence my thinking as a rugby coach and teacher. I realised the need to have a greater range of skills, to help the players to have more options in the tactical game. Hence my belief that it is important to spend more time in warm ups on ball and movement skills. This is especially important for young people of today who seem to have less time for free play away from adult interference.

This rugby experience was to be my last one as a National Serviceman. I had to move on to a permanent posting. My destination was MEAF! I had not heard of the place. It was apparently the abbreviation of Middle East Air Force. My posting was to Aden in Yemen. This city near the base of the Red Sea endured temperatures in the summer of over 40 degrees. I became the typist for the Commanding Officer of RAF Seedaseer. A two-day flight including an overnight stop in Malta and refuelling in Khartoum, eventually saw me arrive in the port city of Aden. I had only ever been from Wales to England twice during my school days. Now I was on another continent. It provided an extremely hot and humid climate with hardly a blade of grass in sight. Sand and rock stretched for miles, with an extinct volcano the dominant feature overlooking the city.

My rugby career was on hold. Instead, I played for the station's football team as an adventurous left back. In the hot season I played for the cricket team. The football scene in Aden was interesting. Our station's team played fixtures against the few other military stations in Aden. More interesting were the games against local Yemeni sides. These players did not wear boots. They were highly skilled and controlled the ball with a high degree of fine touch and finesse. Their lack of leather boots was not a handicap on the hard-packed desert sands. I took many kicks on my shins where the bruises lasted for days. The biggest difference between the teams was our organisation, a very British quality, that perhaps has too often stifled our tactical flexibility in major games, such as football and rugby.

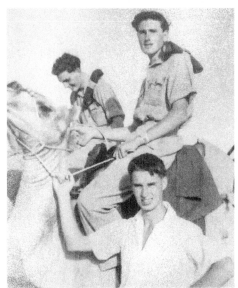

Part of the camel riding group at the RAF Camp in Aden in the Yemen while on my Middle East posting 1957-58

The Arab inhabitants were not hamstrung by organised training sessions. They just played on whatever pieces of solid sand were available. Their instinctive play enabled them to experiment with their skills and without knowing it become more adaptable in the game. Not a blade of grass in sight. Aden was dominated by an extinct volcano. While playing cricket in Aden in the oppressive humidity and heat, I experienced a stoppage in play that could never occur in the U.K. Our side were fielding. I was keeping wicket, always trying to improve my range of skills. The air suddenly started to cool. The sky darkened. An eerie silence descended. One of my slip fielders said, 'I think we should get off the field pretty quickly'. I could see nothing visible approaching. Then, over the headland, a massive dark cloud appeared. In what seemed like an instant, the cloud enveloped the pitch. We began to race for the shelter of the pavilion. Within seconds visibility was zero. Grains of sand stinging my face, it was a frightening experience. The noise of wind and sand whipping around increased in intensity. Only the shouting of the players near the pavilion helped guide me to safety. Sandstorm stopped play!

The barracks in which thirty airmen lived had no air conditioning, only fans. Ever one to learn new skills, I did manage to ride a camel, over which I had no control. While meandering along the beach a passing inhabitant produced a long stick and whacked my camel on the backside. It instantly took off at great speed and threw me forward. I clung desperately on to the camel's neck as he careered along the beach. The Arabic for slow down was not in my vocabulary. A very scary experience all round. I waited until tiredness slowed him down. Then the camel wandered down the beach and into the Yemeni Army's officers' mess. That was the camel's normal resting place. One of the few advantages of my posting in Aden, was the two weeks' annual leave granted. I took this leave in Mombasa, on the beautiful Nyali Beach in Kenya. At this time, it was a white sandy beach

Skiffle Group with home-made instruments Billet 14 RAF Seedaseer Lines Aden the poor man's Lonny Donegan group

with no hotels. There were just a few native huts with basic facilities and an army canteen. The leave time allowed us to explore the city of Mombasa, coupled with excursions inland to the Tsavo Game Reserve. Many airmen spent the two weeks in the company of local ladies, as the social scene in Aden was not exactly buzzing. Our return flight from Aden to Mombasa took us via Somalia, for a fuel stop at Mogadishu. After the heat and humidity of Aden, the cool breezes of the Mombasa coast were a welcome relief. The British Army had taken control of our station

Headquarters RAF Sharjah Persian Gulf where I was the CO's typist!

from the RAF. It was preparing to conduct operations against the so-called 'rebels' in North Yemen. I took the opportunity to fly up country to visit the area where the fighting was taking place. A Pembroke light aircraft was my mode of flight. The scenery on the flight showed that Yemen was not all barren. Deep green valleys, surrounded by rocky mountains, set a stunning scene. I was due to return to Aden in the evening but was off-loaded to enable a pregnant woman to go to the hospital in Aden. I stayed overnight in a tent in the very cold mountains. The journey home next day, in an RAF Beverley transport, that could take off and land in what seemed a minimal amount of space, was another unique experience for me. I marvelled at the sight of the aircraft landing on a sand airstrip on top of the mountain in less than two hundred yards. I just hoped the take-off would be as efficient because the mountain dropped precipitously at the runway's end.

I learned to swim in this heavily salted pool in RAF Sharjah it was impossible to sink!

Several months later, in October 1957, I received notice of one last posting to RAF Sharjah. This base was very close to Dubai in the United Arab Emirates.

I served the rest of my National Service at Sharjah. I visited Dubai frequently. This small port was only five miles away and contained a few streets and bazaars. On our shopping visits, we began to master the practice of haggling for cheaper prices for our tax-free watches and cameras. Who would have foreseen the changes that have turned Dubai into the incredible city it now is? I was not to know that I would return on several occasions to coach in Dubai in local schools. I visited in my role as coach educator for the Penguins International Coaching Academy and also attended the well-established Dubai Rugby Sevens. My football and cricket skills continued to develop in this Persian Gulf outpost. I learned to swim in the station's swimming pool. The water had the density of the salty Dead Sea. It was impossible to sink. This newly acquired skill was to prove beneficial in my future P.E. training as swimming was to become part of the core curriculum.

In terms of developing my playing and coaching during my National Service, there were not many opportunities to develop rugby other than during the basic training times. The standard of back play I experienced then told me that pace was not my strength. Therefore, improving skills and tactical understanding were to be my way forward. I had to think innovatively and trust my Welsh background of rugby based on game play that would enable me to play at a higher level. The nicknames I acquired later in rugby such as 'Wizard', 'Magician' and 'Jinker', but never 'Pacy', perhaps told a tale.

In late July 1958, I received notice of repatriation and demobilisation to the U.K. This was not before I travelled first class in a civilian aircraft, via Entebbe in Uganda including an overnight stop in a four-star hotel with a swimming pool. This proved a relaxing end to my military adventures. My teacher-training awaited me in Exeter, after a short break to reunite with family and friends.

TEACHER TRAINING

'It was a question of having one's faith restored in the aesthetic and artistic qualities of back play'
Carwyn James after watching Hugo Porta (Fly Half Argentina in 1980)

The Fishguard to Penzance express train glided into Newport station early one morning in September 1958. On board were over fifty young Welsh students. Some were returning to continue their teacher training. Others, like me, were about to start their training at St. Luke's College in Exeter.

A very high percentage of those students were rugby players of considerable ability. The Principal of the College pursued a strategy of publicising the college's name, through the exciting and ambitious playing style of the college's rugby teams. The first team at St Luke's had an impressive fixture list, playing many of the first-class teams in England and Wales at that time, among them Llanelli and Bristol. Several international players had played in the rugby team. They included Bryn Meredith of Newport, Wales and the Lions, Gareth Griffiths, Cardiff and Wales and Benny Jones, Pontypool, Devon and Welsh trialist. The group of international players increased in number in this year and subsequent years

My main subjects for training as a teacher were Physical Education and History. At the same time, three fellow students from Pontywaun Grammar School

First year PE students at St. Luke's College Exeter with fellow Welshman Lloyd Worthington next to me chewing his thumbs.

commenced their studies at the college. In my college hostel, I roomed with a young man from Abercarn, Mal Gibbon, who was to become a lifelong friend. Mal's father was the legendary full back Gerry Gibbon, who was playing for Newbridge RFC, one of the top Welsh sides. In the first-year rugby trials, over eighty players attended. There were only three college teams. Many of these triallists were schoolboy internationals. My chance of making one of the teams was very slim. I did not make the squads. So, with a few of my friends, we started playing outside the college for the Paignton first team. Many Devon clubs took advantage of playing the students, who invariably strengthened their squads. During vacations at Christmas and Easter, I would play for Risca, in order to gain experience in the adult game. My home club was very supportive of its student members. Expenses provided for students were generous.

The Principal of the College, Jim Smeall, was a remarkable man. His aim was to make the college stand out as a place of excellence for teacher training. He achieved this partly through the publicity generated by the success of the college's first XV. He succeeded in attracting outstanding students not only to the Physical Education programme, but to subjects across the curriculum. During my time at the college, present and future internationals included; H.J.C. 'John' Brown, RAF and the British Lions, Brian (Ben) Price, Newport and Wales, Graham Hodgson, Neath and Wales, John Scott, Cardiff and England, Martin Underwood, Northampton and England, and my fellow Pontywaunite, Mick Pay together with Luke's hooker Andy Johnson, had many seasons with Northampton.

Students gained honours in other sports. In cricket, Dave Shepherd, a prodigious hitter, played for Gloucestershire and later became a charismatic international umpire. Dave's Devon folklore was evident in his 'Nelson' gesture. Every time the scoreboard displayed the same three numbers, for example, 111, he would perform a swift shuffle on the spot, as a sign of good luck. A fellow student of mine, Roger Self, became manager of the Great Britain hockey team that won a gold medal in

St. Luke's cricket team toured Guernsey 1957. It rained before we got to the square so no play.

the Seoul Olympics. One of the outstanding PE lecturers, Dave Edgecombe, was a one-man Devon Championship athlete, appearing in the National Championships in more than five events.

It was in this environment, that I honed my knowledge of teaching and coaching. The lecturers and fellow students continually challenged you to maintain and increase your standards. I met my future wife, Mary, in Exeter. She was training to be a nurse in the local orthopaedic hospital. Our first meeting was a result of one Saturday night on the town in the Dickens Bar in Exeter. Tipsy romantic student meets nurse! He also avoids meeting her father after walking her home.

Just after I left the College, in 1961, the New Zealand All Blacks came on one of their long tours of the British Isles. They played Newport early on in the tour. A

St.Luke's College first XI 1960. Me sitting on the floor (left). Fellow Welshman and Welsh amateur footballer Graham Reynolds top row second from the right.

St Luke's student, John (Dickie) Uzzell, played for Newport against the All Blacks, along with two of my St Luke's contemporaries, their captain Brian Price and prop Nev Johnson. On a typically wet and windy Welsh afternoon, Newport pulled off a remarkable win, through a dropped goal by none other than Dickie Uzzell. The problem for Dickie was that he had not asked the Principal for permission to play. Next morning, on returning to Exeter, Dickie was 'invited' to explain his unauthorised absence. A stern looking Jim Smeall said nothing for what seemed an eternity to Dickie. Then he smiled at Dickie and said, 'That dropped goal just about saved you from a suspension. Well done but please ask next time!'

At the end of my first term, the college first XI football team, who played in the very competitive Exeter and District League, were looking for a full back to play against Barnstaple. Most students had left on Christmas vacation. One of the first team knew that I played football and asked me to play. I accepted this invitation with delight. After the game, which I think we drew, my team-mates thought I had

Fellow St. Luke's students around the college pool.
Best friend Mal Gibbon (Abercarn) third from left in the back row.

a decent game and encouraged me to play the next term. My football career was back on track.

I also played some cricket for the College's third XI. In one game, our wicketkeeper was a prop forward called 'Tess' O'Shea, who went on to play rugby for Cardiff, Wales and the Lions. Playing on cricket pitches in rural Devon had its hazards. On one occasion, fresh cow pats had been deposited in many parts of the outfield. My best memory of Tess was his diving to try and catch a ball and landing square on a fresh Devonian cowpat. After that incident, the slip cordon disappeared.

The second year of my teacher-training was particularly important as there was more attention to detail. Lecturers encouraged us to take several National Governing Body coaching awards. These included awards in cricket, hockey and athletics. Rugby, at this time, had not introduced coaching awards. We learned to teach the so-called minor sports of judo, boxing and volleyball alongside the major sports.

Gymnastics, swimming and athletics were the core subjects for the PE curriculum. Gaining qualifications and knowledge in this wide range of sports and activities would provide a broad foundation for a PE curriculum in our future schools.

The third year of specialisation was probably the most important. We studied our physical education programme in much greater depth than in the first two years. The programme in the first years concerned the general side of education, including child development and classroom management. The PE group of around sixty post-graduate students regarded themselves as an elite within the college. They were expected to set high standards of dress code, study, teaching practice and in general contributions to the life of the college.

I rang the church bells at morning prayers quite often. I found this to be a pleasant task, and a precursor to succeeding to be accepted on the post-graduate course! I continued to play football for the college. A challenging teaching practice in Plymouth proved enjoyable. I was teaching mostly athletics, under the watchful eye of a very empathetic head of PE. A special memory of my teaching practice in Plymouth was a visit to the local theatre, to see the great Ella Fitzgerald in concert. What a magnificent voice she possessed.

At the close of the spring term in my final year of training, I returned to Risca to play in the deciding game for first place in the Monmouthshire League Rugby Championship. We played this crunch decider against Blaina, on their ground. The village of Blaina was a real heartland of rugby near the head of our valley, A crowd of over one thousand people were watching. This was one of the most competitive and combative games I ever played. I now knew what real valley rugby was about. No-one gave a quarter anywhere on the field. For a young, inexperienced player, this was a rugby education for which no coaching can prepare you. The result was a 3 – 3 draw and my first ever trophy of an engraved shield, still proudly living on my bedside table. I then went on my first Easter rugby tour with Risca, to the far west of Wales, near Pembroke Dock. There was no such game as a 'friendly' in Wales, as I discovered when catching a high ball under my posts. After I passed the ball, an opposing player drove me into one of the posts. When I staggered to my feet, my team mates were pounding the villain in a massive punch-up. The forwards protected the backs in such circumstances.

First year PE students at the College along with PE staff. I am on extreme right second row.

Every Easter vacation, I returned to Risca. I always played in the holiday matches arranged over the weekend. Club rugby was a huge learning experience for a young student fly-half. There were always older and more experienced players waiting to 'put you in your place', by whatever means they could. In a game like rugby, learning to look after your personal safety and finding out what works best, progressed well in the cauldron-like atmosphere of a game. The Welsh valley teams provided those opportunities. You learned not just to survive but also to become more street-wise, by using your burgeoning range of skills of evasion and kicking. The side-step and dummy were two such weapons.

How did my teacher training time at St Luke's College prepare me, not just for a teaching career but also for a future as a rugby coach? The three leading colleges training physical education teachers (males) were Loughborough College, Carnegie College Leeds and St. Luke's. All three colleges provided a specialist diploma in PE that entailed a concentrated, additional, course for one year. This course provided a range and depth of knowledge in more sports than was available in the general two-year teaching qualification. Boxing and volleyball featured alongside the major sports. Gymnastics, swimming and athletics continued to be the core PE subjects. The standards set by the Head of Department, Jock Campbell, were considerably higher than in the two years' course. There was a sense of an elitism, in the best possible way. He required students to set the best possible standards in dress, performance and attitude. A St. Luke's third year student had to present the picture of a college that would set the highest possible standard of teaching available. Students on teaching practice were scrutinised in the quality of their lesson planning, with most first lesson plans returned for improvement. The content of the practical sessions presented to the students included up to date research methods. I was very proud to have had the opportunity of studying at St Luke's. The high level of tutoring we received in Exeter did prepare me for coaching in whatever sport I chose to coach.

Turning to a more social aspect at Luke's, I had learned the skills of conducting a choir, as a result of attending the 'compulsory' rugby players regular pub Saturday night singing. No shouting allowed! This skill was to prove as important as any diploma, as I introduced singing after matches to all teams that I played in or coached ever since. When touring with the Oxford University Rugby football Club in Japan the OURFC choir won many admirers with our generous hosts. Singing, in my opinion, was, and can be conducive to building team spirit.

The influence of St. Luke's College on the PE programmes in schools was considerable. Students with the additional third year training were sought after by schools wishing to develop their physical education programmes. Career pathways to elite positions with national associations attracted many ex-students. I refer to a few examples of the students who went on to secure work in the elite sections of British sport. Don Rutherford, who played for Gloucester, England and the British Lions, became the first Director of Rugby Coaching for the RFU. Don laid the foundations to enable England to become the world-leader in coaching publications in the late sixties, seventies and eighties. Rugby player Mike Rafter became an England rugby international, Gloucestershire coach and administrator in the international game. While another Welshman George Morgan, a modest rugby player from Sengenydd, developed both administrative and diplomatic skills to become President of the Welsh Rugby Union. Graham Reynolds, a Wales amateur international soccer player and Glamorgan cricket all-rounder, became a highly respected talent scout for elite Welsh cricket and football teams.

The college has a very impressive list of alumni who have represented their countries at the highest levels in the game. Those players have made and continue to make significant contributions to both the playing of the game, the coaching and the administration. This team below is just a representation of the quality of players who have contributed to their countries and to the international game.

Some team!

15. Don Rutherford (Gloucester, England & Lions) *

14. Mike Slemen (Liverpool, England & Lions)

13. Gareth Griffiths (Cardiff, Wales & Lions)

12. John 'JC' Brown (RAF & Lions)

11. Martin Underwood (Northampton, England & Lions)

10. John Bevan (Aberavon and Wales)

9. Richard Hill (Bath & England) *

1. John 'Tess' O'Shea (Cardiff, Wales, & Lions)

2. Bryn Meredith (Newport, Wales & Lions) *

3. David Sole (Scotland & Lions) *

4. Danny Harris (Pontypridd & Wales)

5. Brian Price Newport, Wales & Lions) *

6. John Scott (Cardiff & England)

7. Mike Rafter) Bristol and England)*

8. Jeff Squire (Pontypool, Wales and Lions) *

* Captained their national team

Many former PE students of the college became lecturers at teacher training establishments. These included former England rugby winger, Martin Underwood (at St Luke's College) and Leighton Davies, a top-level flanker with Bridgend (at Cardiff College). Martin continued to provide contributions to coaching at international levels long after his playing career finished. My contribution to high-level coaching took a longer route. The invitation, in 1980, to coach Oxford University's rugby team, was a special honour for me.

UNIVERSITY OF EXETER INSTITUTE OF EDUCATION

TEACHER'S CERTIFICATE

Lynn Robert Evans

*has satisfactorily completed a course of training for
the teaching profession at*

Saint Luke's College, Exeter

Principal of College

Director of the Institute of Education

August 1, 1960
Date

Vice-Chancellor of the University

My treasured teaching qualification

It was now time for me to move on for my first teaching position, in a school situated near the iconic city of Oxford. I had secured a post in a newly built, co-educational grammar school, at Littlemore, a large village on the eastern side of the city.

TEACHING

'I try to think how the player is seeing the situation on the field and not what the
detached view the coach is observing.'
Iain McGeehan – British Lions Coach

It was late in the summer term of my final year at St. Luke's College. I had
not yet secured a teaching position. One interview, back in my home county of
Monmouthshire, had led me to a certain amount of disillusion with impartiality in
the interview process. A fairly distinguished group of young, aspiring PE students
applied for the position of boys PE teacher at Cymparc Secondary Modern School.
This group included Berwyn Jones, a Welsh Commonwealth Games sprinter, and
candidates from Loughborough and Carnegie, two leading colleges in physical
education. None of us really had much of a chance. I discovered this after a conversation with the one candidate I knew. Dai Williams, commonly known as 'Dai
Fat', was a local boy from the Newport area, who played for Newport RFC. Dai
confided to me that he was almost certain to get the position, as vacancies in the
county were few and far between. None other than the county PE adviser had
assured him he would be appointed. At that time, all advertisements for positions
in Wales carried a notice 'Any canvassing will disqualify you from this position'. I
collected my expenses and headed for jobs in England.

I applied for the post of temporary PE teacher at a grammar school in Littlemore village, close to the city of Oxford. Being close to a beautiful city like Oxford
and the prospect of working in a grammar school appealed to me. On arriving for
interview, in early July 1961, at this newly built mixed grammar school on the edge
of a housing estate, I found the school empty of pupils. They had all gone away
for day trips around the country. The headteacher who interviewed me, Ben Halliday, was one of the most forward-thinking headteachers I had the good fortune
to work under. I was the only candidate, which was quite encouraging. He offered
the position to me and I accepted it. When Ben found out that my return train to
Newport was several hours away, he invited me to his home for tea. That must be
a first for any interviewee.

I greatly appreciated Ben's care and support during the early years of my teaching career. He provided most of the furniture in my first rented schoolhouse in
Benson, outside Oxford. He was extremely enthusiastic about introducing rugby
in the school. This would entail considerable expense. New pitches and new rugby
equipment would be required. Ben did not see any problems and managed to have
everything in place by the start of the new school year. I had to have the Welsh col-

ours somewhere in the scheme. Accordingly, the new Littlemore GS rugby shirts were red and white stripes. At this period in the early sixties, a considerable number of rugby-playing Welsh teachers headed to England for employment. I suppose the term Welsh rugby missionaries could apply, but that might appear to be rath-

First ever rugby team at Littlemore Grammar school in Oxford

er pretentious. In more and more schools in England, qualified teachers taught rugby. In the Oxfordshire town of Wantage, around ten primary school teachers were Welsh rugby players. In the early seventies, their passion for the game saw them form a rugby club in Grove, a new housing development on the outskirts of the town.

On arriving at the school in September 1961, the rugby posts were up, the lines marked, and the school rugby shirts had arrived. I began to look for suitable fixtures for the next school year. There were already football fixtures to honour during the first year. What I saw in the school football team was a group of all-round games players, perfect fodder to learn rugby. Curricular time during both winter terms would involve teaching rugby. I was applying the principle of overload.

Littlemore was a 'football area'. The older students were not all enthusiastic about rugby. The new intake, like most eleven-year olds, were keen to play any sport. Without the voluntary support of other teachers in the school, we would have been unable to run teams in the lower school. I was fortunate that during the 1960s, teachers were enthusiastic to take a role in extra-curricular activities. This volunteering entailed taking the teams on a Saturday morning to schools spread across Oxfordshire and neighbouring counties. If the games were at home, then they had to referee the match. Sadly, Saturday morning fixtures in state schools today rarely exist. Extra administrative duties take up an ever-increasing amount of teachers' time.

During the late 60s, it was possible to play adult rugby players against school teams, especially former pupils of the school against the current school first XV.

Winners of section 3 for smaller schools in the U18 prestigious Sevens tournament on the Oxfordshire Sevens. Coached by local rugby guru Charlie Ede.

A student teacher at the school, just happened to be doing his Post Graduate Certificate in Education at Oxford University. Ken Jones (DK as he was known) was a Welsh International and future British Lion. Ken suggested he could bring a team to play the school's first team. The game provided an opportunity to raise money for a school charity. The impressive team he chose included some local county level players. He brought over half the university Blues squad including the Scottish international duo of full back Stuart Wilson and charismatic centre, Joe McPartlin. The whole school came out to watch the spectacle. The game was played in a great spirit. The invitational side, mostly, allowed for the inexperience

Michael Tanner Littlemore Grammar school interviews student teacher D. K. (Ken) Jones Llanelli, Wales and British Lions.

of the school players. The skills and class on display by the invitational side was evident. I am sure, the school first XV players would remember this special game for the rest of their lives.

Within three years, the rugby had developed to an extent that fixtures took place against established rugby playing schools. A rugby sevens programme began in the Spring Term, with the assistance of Charles Ede, a local sevens enthusiast. Charlie, as he was affectionately known, was the founder of a midweek team in the city known as Oxford Thursday. This team effectively served as a recruiting agency for future membership of Oxford RFC. I made my debut for the Thursdays, within a week of meeting Charlie, against the Harwell Atomic Research team. Charlie was unashamedly, the 'chief scout' for the city of Oxford Rugby Club.

Among the group that constituted the first ever LGS senior team, was Michael Tanner. He became the first pupil from the school to be accepted as a student at Oxford University. His choice of college was a wise one. St. Edmund Hall had established a reputation as Oxford's senior rugby college. Michael went on to play for the university team, the Dark Blues, over forty times during his stay in residence. He was extremely unlucky not to win the coveted Blue. Players gain a rugby Blue through representing the university in the annual fixture at Twickenham against Cambridge University. His rival for the scrum half position happened to be the current New Zealand All Blacks number 9, Chris Laidlaw. I had the pleasure of playing outside Mike, as his fly-half for Oxford City, while he was still at school. He looked after me!

In the late sixties, our sevens programme was beginning to achieve success. In the local Oxfordshire sevens tournament, which was effectively a national competition for schools, we achieved considerable success. Our U16 team won the section for smaller schools, with a memorable last-minute try, to overcome a powerful Howardian High School from Cardiff. The U18 team achieved success, playing some scintillating sevens, to overcome St. Benedict's College, a leading public school. In that side, we had Ian Ray, one of the most talented athletes I had the pleasure of teaching. Ian was an all-round sportsman, who represented the Oxford Boys U15 representative football team, the county rugby team and eventually the national England U15 team. His prowess extended to representing Oxfordshire at the All England National Schools Athletics championship in four very different events, in four separate years. He ran in the 100m, 400m, and competed in the long jump and shot putt competitions. Ian went on to become a star sevens player with Richmond RFC, appearing in several Middlesex national sevens tournaments.

A new experience for the players at the school was the time-honoured desire of most rugby players, to go on a tour. There was no better place to start than where

(Left) Littlemore G.S. first rugby tour to Besancon in France and Bern in Switzerland. 1968
(Right) The touring team in France of Littlemore GS

I had lived, the Ebbw Valley stretching from Newport to Brynmawr. I contacted the rugby teacher at Bassaleg GS, a former neighbour of mine Askey Harris from Risca. We arranged a two-fixture weekend tour to play against his school and Newbridge GS. Stuart Barnes, former Oxford University, Newport, Bristol, Bath and England player, and now rugby correspondent at The Times, attended Bassaleg. He won a number of Welsh 18 Group international caps at full back. The tour was planned around Ian Ray's first international appearance as fly-half for

*(Left) The touring team in France enjoying the delights of Bern in Switzerland
(Right) Jerry Smith, LGS captain, leads the team against Besconsan. We were described on posters in the
town as Oxford University Juniors!*

England 15 group against Wales at Cardiff Arms Park, the home of Welsh Rugby. His school's first team were there to cheer him on. Wales won!

We had selected in the touring team Seretse Williams, a very gifted and versatile player of West Indian descent. Seretse was a three-quarter who could play in most positions in the backs. He had just turned fifteen. As we arrived at Bassaleg, the school situated just outside Newport, the head of rugby Askey, approached me as he had watched Seretse, exit the coach. He said 'I am sure it will be alright. As you know, we don't see many black people down here, but he is with a lovely family.' Askey was a super guy, and his words brought home to me the vast cultural differences between Oxford and the valleys of South Wales. West Indians had not yet ventured that far west. In our second tour match, at Newbridge, Seretse played full back. Newbridge was a traditionally strong rugby school. I knew its team would adopt a combination of ambitious Welsh handling and a streetwise tenacity, typical of valley adult teams. The Littlemore boys would not be accustomed to playing against such a team. Here was a small boy, full back, in an exposed position! Very early on, up went the kick to Seretse. I said a little prayer, as two opponents were bearing down on him with intent. He caught the ball under pressure, swayed his hips, unbalancing the first defender, neatly side-stepping the second one, and then found a thirty-metre touch kick. An elderly Welsh supporter standing next to me, took a puff on his pipe, and muttered, 'That's class!'. Intuitive play is not just a gift of the Welsh, I thought. We lost both games but not by great margins. Many of the boys commented to me that the games were more intensive that the ones they played back home. I realised that I had been playing club rugby in the

Swimming teacher! Peers School.

latter stages of my school career. The chances of playing club rugby in England at such a young age, were not so available. During this period in the 60s, Keith Jarrett, a player from Monmouth School for Boys, played his first international match for Wales against England at full back. Just eighteen years of age, he was a sensation, scoring nineteen points in a winning debut.

A second tour was to follow. This time, Littlemore travelled to foreign lands, as Oxfordshire Education Authority had established links with the Jura region in eastern France. In 1974, a colleague of mine, Bob Martin, a modest rugby player but passionate rugby tourist, arranged a three-game tour over two weeks in late August. We played games against teams from the towns of Besancon, Dole and Lons le Sonnier. It was the beginning of my long association with French rugby. Two minibuses, one a redundant fish van, set out on our rugby adventure. The U18 team encountered new and daunting experiences. They met opponents, many of whom had longer than average facial hair. The opposing teams had as many substitutes as players. Welcome to French rugby! The referees allowed liberal interpretations of the laws of rugby. Very quickly, I learned that we were in a very different rugby culture, with passionate and friendly people. Every team had arranged a pre-match Mayoral reception, with local wine being abundantly available. This posed a social challenge for our staff of three adults! At least, the players were denied pre-match drinks! The touring experience in this part of France left me wanting to know more about the rugby set up in the country. This was to happen several years later. We won our three games, with the players being first class ambassadors for our school. We had been advertised in the local press as 'Oxford University Juniors', with a five French francs entry fee for our matches. I reasoned that Littlemore GS had achieved a new status. We even managed to visit a cinema on our return via Paris, showing the then risqué film, Emmanuelle. I tried hard to stay awake. It was only when the music started that woke me up. Littlemore GS was to experience two special events concerning New Zealand rugby. The head of New Zealand coach development, Bill Freeman a renowned thinker on rugby, was doing an invited tour of England. He conducted coaching sessions for coaches. Oxfordshire RFU chose Littlemore GS as a venue for one of his clinics. I offered our facilities as we possessed some mobile floodlighting, a rare commodity in those days. Over one hundred coaches attended Bill's session which dealt with the concepts of rucking. Bill's clear and precise approach to the coaching of effective rucking impressed me. The school first team's smaller than average sized pack of forwards would go on to utilise the ruck as a potent weapon of winning quick ball. The team's ball retention from the ruck was more efficient against our more physical opponents. Our skilled threequarters consequently had a few bits of quicker ball with which to play.

In 1972, the All Blacks were on a tour to the UK. During this tour they played a game in Oxford against a select Southern Counties team. The All Blacks were playing basically their second-string team, as the Counties were not among their hardest opposition. The New Zealand management team wanted some activity

(Left) With friend John Batey on the LGS tour to France at Lons le Sonier
(Right) At Crystal Palace National Sports centre for a week long sports course with three local Oxford Schools

for players not involved in the game. They required an indoor gym for basketball. Lynn Evans had a new gym at his school. Yes, they were very happy to come but could I referee a basketball game between their forwards and backs? This basketball game turned out to be one of the hardest refereeing experiences of any sport that I had refereed. Cheating (or testing the referee's resolve) was, and maybe still is, endemic in the New Zealand player. Some call it competitiveness! They hate losing. Watching the diminutive scrum half Sid Going and flying wing Bryan Williams taking on huge forwards like Colin Meads and Brian Lochore was an education for me. The game resembled half basketball and half rugby. I knew now why they were hard to beat. They hated losing at anything. Most decisions I made were questioned by the other team. The players though did thank me at the end of the game. The pupils at the school scored heavily on the autograph front.

As the Littlemore GS teams developed, we secured fixtures against the independent schools in Oxford city, namely Magdalen College, Southfield, and eventually St. Edward's School. To play competitively against these larger schools our rugby had to have a more adventurous and fluid style. This was mainly because winning primary possession in scrum and lineout was a problem. If the weather

Clearing the stream while testing the cross-country course at Peers School!

conditions were unfavourable, with wind and rain, the team had to ensure we did not waste our minimal possession. The ball retention skills needed to be superior to our opponents.

I became involved in the county rugby set-up and invited to coach the U18 group team. I organised a pre-season camp at Radley College, just outside Oxford, where potential county players attended a week-long course. This coaching week enabled me to start thinking about the role of more intensive coaching and its possible impact on a player's long-term development. At this time, these types of training camps were rare, as funding was limited. The support of the county's Physical Education adviser, Arthur Cox, was vital to obtain such funding. Arthur was very keen for the more talented sportspeople to receive coaching of high quality. These camps served a useful purpose in helping the young players bridge the gap between school and senior sport. My younger daughter, Cressida, attended courses over four years in volleyball, netball and tennis. In rugby, we concentrated on improving technical and tactical skills, combined with an appropriate fitness programme. Several other major sports held their programmes at the same time. I found conversations with coaches, who were all teachers, from the other sports, very beneficial. We exchanged views on our varying approaches to coaching. These county 'Schools of Sport' played a significant part in players' development. Better coaching for potential county players benefits their performance at the higher levels.

I experienced some unique educational opportunities at the school. Every year, for ten years, I accompanied a group of senior boys on a two-week outdoor pursuit visit to Patterdale Hall, near Ullswater, a centre owned by Oxfordshire County Council in the Lake District. During the third year of the visit, Littlemore Grammar School became the first school in the County to have a mixed boys and girls group taking part in an outdoor pursuits course. The extremely rigorous course that involved mountaineering, rowing, rock climbing and orienteering, showed that girls could emulate boys in these demanding activities. The adult leaders of the course were so impressed with the performances of the girls that they confirmed that future courses for girls would continue. This was quite an achievement in those conservative times.

Another memorable event occurred when Archbishop Desmond Tutu of South Africa was on a visit to Oxford. He was attending a special presentation at the school's sports hall. Somehow, he arrived on his own at the reception area of the centre, where I was waiting for the official party to arrive. He bounded over to me with that infectious smile he had. He wanted to know what I did at the school and continued a conversation for several minutes, before the main party arrived. He exuded charm, enthusiasm and compassion. He showed himself to be a special human being.

A pleasure of teaching, during the seventies and early eighties, was the freedom PE teachers had to broaden the curriculum. There were concerns, even in those times, about the fitness and lifestyle of children in the UK. After conversations

LGS U.16 Sevens team winners of Oxon tournament against Howardian HS Cardiff

with the county PE adviser, we decided to promote a health-related programme into the curriculum. Arthur gave his approval for the construction of an outdoor circuit training course around the perimeter of the extensive school playing fields. In conjunction with Loughborough Colleges, who were producing fitness diaries for use in schools, I introduced a health-related fitness programme. Tim Brighouse, a visionary educator and Oxfordshire Director of Education, performed the official opening of the fitness trail. Tim came early to the official opening and asked for a guided tour of the new facility. He was passionately interested in the scheme, as he fired question after question to me. He was concerned about greater physical activity for children in the education programme in schools.

Another remarkable Welshman called Malcolm Elias joined the physical education department in 1972. He hailed from the rugby nursery in Wales, namely Llanelli Grammar School. He loved rugby but loved football even more. His main extra-curricular role was to develop and produce successful football teams. He also played a full part in broadening the curriculum to allow the pupils to explore new activities. During the fifteen years in which we taught together, the school U16 team reached the latter stages of the National Cup competition no fewer than six times. Quite an achievement with the quality of opposition we faced nationally. Four boys went on to play for the local professional team Oxford United. One Mark Wright, went further, playing for Liverpool and England. Malcolm left teaching to pursue a career as a youth scout in football for the Oxford team. Within the next twenty years from the late eighties, he became not only a leading recruitment scout in England, but within the top ten scouts worldwide. His scouting expertise quickly became recognised, and he became chief youth scout, firstly for Swansea, his beloved local team in Wales, then Southampton, Liverpool and latterly Fulham. Among the players he 'discovered' and recruited, were Gareth Bale, Real Madrid and Wales, English internationals Theo Walcott, Luke Shaw, Trent-Alexander Arnold, Adam Lallana plus a host of Premier League players. He is at present working with Fulham. The success of that club at age group level has been hugely influenced by Malcolm's shrewd recruitment policy. Among the rising stars at Fulham is another gem, Ryan Sessegnon and his brother. Malcolm was one of the most driven, passionate, hardworking and supportive people I have come across. His success has been well earned.

Sadly, Littlemore Grammar School became the victim of educational change. In the seventies, educational changes were all too frequent. The original buildings are no longer there, except for one building used by Littlemore RFC. The rugby club occupies a former languages classroom, converted into their clubhouse. What irony! Littlemore GS lost its status as a grammar school and many other changes took place over the next fifteen years. The school merged with Northfield Secondary School, who shared the same site, and became Littlemore Associated Schools. Later, the school became known as Peers School, a 13 to 18 upper comprehensive school. The school came under the authority of the City of Oxford, as the boundaries of the city expanded in the late eighties. The city also took control of some other fringe villages.

The impact of some of these changes hit rugby badly. Introducing rugby to thirteen-year olds was to prove very difficult. Thirteen-year-old boys were more resistant to start rugby. My enthusiasm to coach rugby was being tested, as was my enthusiasm and energy to coach some reluctant beginners. There were other challenges I wished to pursue in rugby and other areas of education. There were still occasional rays of light within the general gloom. One of these rays involved Simon Brown, a sixteen-year old who lived with his mother on the nearby Blackbird Leys estate. He had played rugby in curriculum time and also played Colts rugby for Oxford Marathons, a local team. Rugby seemed to centre around his life while he was at the school. Simon had played for Oxfordshire Colts at representative level and was eligible for England Schools Sixteen Group team. The RFU representative for Oxford University, Peter Johnson, was a former Oxford Blue, and a hooker, who taught rugby at the nearby Radley College. I asked him if he could give some scrum tips for Simon before his England trial. Not only did he coach him but offered him a sports scholarship to Radley College. Simon had been due to leave school and start a mechanics apprentice course. He played for England 16 Group and went on to play for England U21. Later, Simon played for the Harlequins in the new professional era. He went on to become a PE teacher locally at Magdalen College School. Later, he became head coach of the prestigious Rugby School's first fifteen, the birthplace of rugby football. The contact network in rugby can have a powerful influence over the direction of a person's future career. It can open doors that might not have previously been available. In 2018, Simon received the award of School Coach of the year in the RFU National Awards. Several other former Littlemore students went on to become PE teachers, some attending my former college in Exeter.

My retirement party at Iffley Road

During my teaching career at Littlemore, including the later years at the re-named Peers Comprehensive school, I realised I had acquired a vast range of skills and experience across many sports. I introduced new sports into the curriculum. These included weight training, basketball, volleyball, tennis, softball, a basic skills PE programme and, importantly for the pupils, a health-related fitness programme.

I saw the value of playing many different games to enable the transfer of skills that had common uses in all the games. The coaching of common key principles, in both skills and tactics, enhances game understanding in all the games. Speciali-sation in one sport at an early age, may not be the best foundation for a longer-term development into adulthood. In my time at the school, I was able to secure a year's secondment for a course in modern educational dance. I will reveal more detail later. Another term on secondment at the Oxford Polytechnic College studying re-search aspects of learning, proved to be another rewarding experience. These im-portant secondments are increasingly rare in teaching, as school budgets decline. I valued greatly the opportunities provided by the head, Ben Halliday, to allow the PE department the freedom to broaden the curriculum. We experimented with the introduction of a variety of activities, including a range of outdoor pursuits, such as mountaineering, canoeing and sailing. The breadth of educational opportunities available, during the sixties and seventies, enabled teachers to provide their stu-dents with new and exciting challenges.

FROM PLAYER TO COACH

'The coach who uses an athlete-centred style of coaching divests himself or herself
of power, however gradually, and shares it with the athletes.'

Kidman, Hadfield and Cho

Within weeks of starting my first job at Littlemore, in 1961, I realised that going
home to play for Risca RFC could not continue. I needed to stay in Oxford as I had
to prepare my lessons for teaching. I also wanted to establish a social life and get to
know people in and around my new home in Oxford.

My introduction to Oxford RFC was quite amusing. I had signed up in a pub
used by the rugby club in the centre of Oxford, called the Kings Arms. This pub
was not only a tourist attraction but also the city base for the Oxford Club. A Welsh
fly half turning up out of the blue, attracted some interest! Nationality sometimes
helps in life!

A friend introduced me to Charlie Ede. He was owner of sundry fish and chip
shops in the Oxford area and a rugby nut! Charlie ran the local midweek side at
that time, called Oxford Thursdays. The team catered for, among others, workers
who had Thursday afternoons off work. Charlie got me a game for the Oxford
club, for the next Saturday. I was to start in the Extra A team, the fourths.

The captain, a very amusing Welshman called Danny Hughes, picked me up
for the away trip to play Newbury B. I was already struggling with the team labels.
In Wales, we had first and second XVs and that was it. In England, some teams
had up to ten teams, Extra Bs and Cs, very complicated. Danny's role as captain
seemed to include being a taxi driver for other ownerless car members of the team.
We toured Oxford picking up the remnants of the side. We arrived thirty minutes
late for kick off. I kicked off long and, as Danny passed me, he said 'You take all the
kicks'. After the game, Danny said you won't be with us for long. I thought there
might be a fifth team! 'By the way, it's three shillings and sixpence'. I replied, 'Oh
thanks Danny, that's handy'. 'No, no' he replied, 'that's match fees for playing'.
That was my welcome to strict amateurism. Maybe I should have stayed in Risca,
where 'expenses' allowed a poor student some social activity at the weekend.

The following week, I made my debut at fly half for the first team. At this time,
Oxford were playing at a level just under the top echelon of club rugby. The team
played a number of fixtures against top Welsh sides of the day, such as, Pontypool,
Neath, Crosskeys, Abertillery and Pontypridd. Fixtures against teams in England
included London Welsh and London Irish and Bedford. Games against teams of

My year as captain of Oxford RFC 1970

similar strength to Oxford took place with the likes of Stroud, Cheltenham, Clifton, Nuneaton, Bridgwater and Barnstaple.

Every Easter, the fixture secretary organised a ritual tour to South Wales with an under-strength team. He provided Welsh clubs with the sacrificial lamb of Oxford RFC. Nevertheless, the tour provided good opportunities to play games at the highest level. The games I enjoyed the most were such as playing Pontypool at Pontypool Park on an Easter Monday morning, in front of crowds numbering in their thousands. I relished the challenge of facing the formidable trio of Price, Windsor and Faulkner, with Welsh scrum half Clive Rowlands operating behind their dominant scrum and the crowd baying for English blood. I was in my home country, near my home of Risca, and always wanted to show how I could play. The flow of adrenalin ensured I was operating near the top end of my game. Games at Crosskeys, where I was quite well known, were the matches in which I tried to show my 'Welshness' had not disappeared because I was resident in England. Sadly for us, we rarely won on our Welsh visits.

My one and only tour to Ireland occurred in my first season at Oxford. A fairly chaotic but thoroughly enjoyable tour of the Republic saw us playing Old Belvedere, a former club of Welsh International Cliff Morgan, Wexford and Lansdowne. The highlight, though, was not the rugby but the tour of the world-famous Guinness factory. A former Irish international, Des O'Brien, who just happened to work for the Ind Coope Brewery in Oxford, arranged this visit. There is a well-established link between beer consumption and rugby.

Every year, the incoming captain of OURFC arranged a pre-term game against Oxford RFC. This provided an opportunity for the captain to assess newcomers to the University, alongside more established players. Captains against whom I played included Charles Kent, a future England captain, Joe McPartlin, a future Scottish international, Bob Phillips, who went on to play for London Welsh with much distinction and Tommy Bedford, a legendary South African flanker. We lost most of these contests. However, on two occasions, the club team managed creditable victories. It was below the dignity of OURFC to label the fixture under the University name. Accordingly, in a very Oxford way, the game featured the University Captain's XV. This ensured that the official fixture records did not contain any of these losses.

The Oxford rugby club attracted many talented rugby players who had moved to the area. The fixture list was of a higher calibre than any of the club teams in Oxfordshire. Many players came from the two main RAF stations, at Abingdon and Benson. A number of newly qualified teachers, especially PE teachers, savoured the delights of the University city.

In the early sixties, the Oxfordshire Rugby Union appointed Geoff Windsor-Lewis as the new captain of the county team. A former Cambridge Blue and a winner of two Welsh International caps, Geoff was to transform the underachieving county team. He was instrumental in improving the selection, preparation and administration of the team. None of the Southern Group of counties (Oxfordshire, Berkshire, Buckinghamshire, Dorset and Wilts) had ever beaten any of the more powerful South-West counties. Within three years after 1963, Oxfordshire were to beat the powerful Gloucestershire team twice. One of these wins occurred at the intimidating bastion of Gloucester RFC, the Kingsholm ground. We gained another victory at Iffley Road, Oxford. It was a privilege for me to play a part in those victories. In the second of these games, at Iffley Road, our scrum half, Nigel Starmer-Smith, an England International, suffered a severe concussion just before half-time. Geoff 'volunteered' me to play in his place. In those days, there were no substitutes. I went on to re-invent the role of the scrum half, mostly through fear and an over production of adrenalin. The between-the-legs pass from the scrum half was a rarity in rugby. It was not the case at Iffley Road that day. I was grateful to our forwards for protecting me. We won that quarter-final game in some style. We lost both semi-finals narrowly. The first loss was to Durham by six points to three. I swear, to this day, that my dropped goal went between the posts. Unfortunately, the ball passed above the

Winners of the inaugural Oxfordshire RFU knockout cup at Iffley Road Oxford

Conducting the Club singing after the Oxon Cup final!

height of the uprights. The referee was unsure and disallowed the goal. County rugby, in those days, was the next level of rugby below the National Team. I learned so much from Geoff's leadership skills and efficient administrative skills. I saw how they enhanced the progress and development of a team. Oxfordshire, during the period of Geoffrey's captaincy, went from under-achievers to over-achievers. He prepared the County team well, tactically and strategically, to meet the challenge of teams that on paper were much stronger.

In 1965, I played for Oxfordshire against Oxford University at Iffley Road. After the game, both teams went for a meal and drinks to Vincent's Club. This was a Members club for sportsmen of the University. After a meal, and while enjoying a few drinks, one of my team members approached me and said 'Do you know the Beatles are drinking downstairs?' I laughed. Then, curiosity getting the better of me, I ventured to the lower bar. Lo and behold the Fab Four were with none other than Jeffrey Archer, politician and author, who, at that time, was studying a postgraduate course at Oxford. The Beatles were attending a Charity dinner at Brasenose College organised by Jeffrey. They enjoyed anonymity here, as no one would find them in this exclusive university club. I persuaded George Harrison to autograph my match programme. The following day I auctioned it at school – for charity! Several weeks later, I invited Jeffrey Archer, as the Secretary of Oxford

Oxford RFC visit to the Guinness factory in Dublin while on Easter tour 1961

University Athletics Club, to present trophies at my school's annual sports day. He was excellent value at the sports day. We shall not cover his political life here.

I went on to captain the Oxford RFC team in the 1966/67 season and again in the 1970/71 season. In my first season as captain, I suffered a dislocated shoulder in the pre-season trials. In a comeback game against Bedford, a few months after the injury, I dislocated the shoulder for a second time. Over the next few seasons, I suffered three more recurring dislocations. Following the last injury that occurred in a County Championship match, I required surgery to secure the joint. If successful, this would enable me to continue playing, much to the concern of my wife. The launch of the inaugural Oxfordshire Knock-out Cup came, during my captaincy, in the 70/71 season. Teams throughout England played cup rugby for the first time. Oxford comfortably reached the final and played this against Henley at Iffley Road, in late April. We became the first winners of the Cup, beating the second strongest side in the county. There was much celebrating and singing, with yours truly as conductor, at Oxford's Southern By-Pass Ground.

Alongside my playing career, I was continuing to develop my coaching career. I assisted Peter West, the first 'real coach', at the Oxford club. I was now attending many of the in-service coaching courses organised by the RFU. Don Rutherford (ex-St. Luke's, Gloucester and England) was head of the newly formed RFU Coach Development Scheme. During this period, in the late 60s and 70s England led the world in the production of new coaching material and providing education courses for coaches. I was fortunate to be part of this revolution in coaching.

In 1972, I attended a conference, in London, entitled, 'When the Lions Speak'. The main speakers were the British Lions coach Carwyn James and the captain, John Dawes. Carwyn's contribution influenced my thinking about rugby and how to change our approach to coaching to resemble what was already under way at London Welsh RFC.

During the 60s and 70s, Pontypool RFC had the most feared and organised set of forwards of that generation. On occasions, their legendary rolling maul would move forward at distances of 30 to 50 metres. At the peak of their efficiency they played Cardiff at Pontypool Park. The Cardiff back division was of a high-quality. However, with the Pontypool pack denying them much ball to play with, they had few opportunities to demonstrate their skills. Pontypool dominated both possession and position on the field. Yet Cardiff won the game with four tries, all scored by the Welsh and Lions wing, Gerald Davies. These tries all began from positions inside the Cardiff half. Cardiff certainly put in an impressive defensive performance that day. It was their ambition and skill in counter-attack that proved to be the difference between the two sides. So much for the modern-day cliché of 'we need to play in the right areas of the field'.

Bisham Abbey national sport centre delivering an RFU Coaching course in 1970s

Coaching at Peers Sports Centre

During the period I was playing County rugby a significant event occurred in Oxford. A team from South Africa, selected by the former Oxford University Captain, and South African captain, Tom Bedford, came to Oxford and played a game against the County team at Iffley Road. The touring party consisted of ten white, ten black and ten coloured players. We must remember this was the age of apartheid in South Africa, and there was no mixed rugby taking place in that country. Tommy had done a remarkable thing by selecting such a group and bringing them on tour to the UK. The result of a win for the Proteas (their team name) over Oxfordshire, must have given Tom and the team great pleasure.

In the late 70s, I took the RFU Senior Coaches Award, held over a weekend at Portsmouth Naval Station. This course certainly tested your knowledge, or lack of it, in a rigorous examination of both theory and practice. Fortunately for me, I was to become closely associated with one of those Staff Coaches, during the weekend. This coach, HV 'Chalky' White, was to have an immense influence on my development as a coach. Chalky was coach to Leicester RFC and regional coach for Midlands select teams when they played against the international touring teams. He became my mentor, friend, adviser and examiner. He advised me of the values of accuracy, precision, strategy and tactics in my coaching. Chalky never left a stone unturned. I always felt on edge, when in conversation with him, as he would often ask, 'What happened next?'. Not suffering fools gladly, he raised the bar for me in coaching, in the best possible way. He contributed significantly to my development as a coach.

I began working with the Oxfordshire Schools Rugby Union in the mid 1960s with their programme for under nineteens. Brian Poxon, another dedicated school-teacher, organised this programme. He was also selector for the English Schools' U15 age-group. Brian's was another extremely supportive influence in providing coaching opportunities for my development. The county organised the first resi-dential coaching course for U19s and held it at Radley College. Funding for this course came via the Physical Education department at County Hall. I was to be the first rugby course leader. I would like to see aspiring rugby coaches follow a less structured career pathway. Instead of relying on coaching awards and 'continual professional development', why not seek out the most innovative and exceptional coaches and 'hang on to their coat tails'. Then start developing yourself.

The most memorable game I played for Oxford RFC was in January 1972. Following the recent launch of the National Knock-Out Cup, Oxford RFC had won the first Oxfordshire Cup. As a result, the team qualified for the Regional and National draws. After winning two regional matches, Oxford now entered the draw in which the first-class clubs participated. Our reward was to play London Welsh away in late January at Old Deer Park in Richmond. This game took place in the same year that I was on a secondment from my teaching post, to study a course in dance.

The British and Irish Lions team had just returned from their successful tour of New Zealand. The team, under the direction of Carwyn James, had defeated the All Blacks for the first time in the Lions' history. The captain of London Welsh was John Dawes, the Lions' captain The London Welsh team contained six Lions who were making their first appearance after returning from New Zealand. John Dawes had already established a style of playing at the Welsh which was innovative and exciting. This playing style involved speed of movement and handling coupled with exceptional levels of ball skills.

Oxford experienced considerable difficulties in this game. I found these out in the first half, when making more tackles in ten minutes than in an entire season. I thought I would pass out. After every tackle the ball would appear far away, as the dynamic Welsh switched play and direction with accuracy and speed. In the second half, I decided to play as near to offside (or offside) as I could, to help stem the tide of attacks. On two occasions I intercepted passes from scrum half Billy Hullin. On the first occasion, I sprinted (using the word somewhat liberally). As I approached the try line, I could hear feet closing in on me. As Gerald Davies, the Lions wing, hit me, I threw a pass to my right where the Oxford fly half Ray Tap-per caught it. Unfortunately, he fumbled the ball, which in those days constituted a knock on. My second interception saw me clear again with only the number 15 to beat. Now, JPR Williams, Wales and the Lions, had a passion for strong tackling. I quickly abandoned thoughts of swerve and sidestep, I settled for the chip kick over JPR's head and subsequent chase. With the adrenalin pumping hard, I slightly over hit my kick. The ball landed in the touch-in-goal area. Our winger, Duncan Kilgour dived on the ball, touched down and slid over the dead ball line. Unfortunately, the referee was somewhere near the halfway line. He took an easy option and ordered a scrum five. He then admonished me for advising him that it could only be a 22 metre drop out or a try. London Welsh's style of playing rugby has stayed with me.

My playing career at the elite end of the game was coming to an end. I had dislocated my shoulder again while playing for Oxford against Guy's Hospital. I received encouraging news from the surgeon who treated me on the field. He said he did not think the shoulder would dislocate again. I was at a stage in my teaching career, when I needed to look at opportunities for new challenges.

I wanted to find out more about how to develop a similar style of play. My journey would take ten years and the intervention of Pierre Villepreux, a visionary French full back and later coach of Toulouse and France.

Meanwhile, my playing career at Oxford was nearing its end. I had resumed playing and enjoyed playing alongside several of my former students from Littlemore Grammar School. Other than Michael Tanner, the students from Littlemore to play with me included Ian Ray, Alan Jenkins (of Welsh heritage) was a

Listening to World Cup referee Ed Morrison delivering on an Oxfordshire Rugby Coaching course

Me with some budding rugby players at Iffley Road

fine hooker who played for Henley. Seretse Williams and Roy Davies, a running machine and tackler, both went on to play first class rugby. I learned from these players that they all had differing strengths. However, all had a determination to make the most of their talents. As a coach, working with young players, I had to gain knowledge about all aspects of the game. It was important to learn about forward-orientated knowledge of the set piece as well as back play and all the generic skills that constitute the game. This grounding has, in my opinion, proved to be a sound way of developing an all-round understanding of the game.

PIERRE VILLEPREUX

'I think it (coaching through game play) is the game of today because as coach I work on the fundamental principles of rugby of going forward and, how to support, where to support, why to penetrate and when to play wide. These decisions are the decisions of the players, not the decision of the coach, and I try to coach that. I try to give the player the liberty and possibility to take the initiative where the other players can see he plays like that.'

Pierre Villepreux – French coach

THE ROLE AND INFLUENCE OF PIERRE VILLEPREUX

Why is Pierre such an exceptional coach and visionary? He studied physical education at university and graduated with top honours. Students who achieve these highest grades often gain paid employment by the French Government in whatever line of education they find work. He was fortunate, at university, to come under the tutelage of Rene Delaplace, a remarkable lecturer. Rene's philosophy on coaching was, in the late sixties and seventies, very different from the directed and coachled methods that prevailed in schools and sports clubs. His vision of teaching and coaching games involved using the game itself as the central tool of learning. He espoused a game-centred approach that involved the player being actively engaged in the learning. He used fundamental concepts that are common to all games in which

With Pierre Villepreux and Des Diamond RFU at RFU conference

74

teams have to score through going into the opponent's territory to secure points or goals. Those principles of going forward and supporting the movement of the ball are similar in such games as basketball, football, hockey, netball and handball. Rene must have inspired Pierre to such an extent that he was to adopt what he had learned and use it throughout his career.

I first met Pierre in 1980 while he was on a coaching visit to the UK. Don Rutherford, the Head of Coaching at the RFU at this time, had organised this visit. The coaching session I observed at Marlow RFC, in August of that year, was, to say the least, unlike any other coaching session I had seen. Pierre was coaching the South Region U17 team. The session focussed on game-centred activity. Players had to find solutions to the challenges set by Pierre in many game situations. My 'untrained' eyes struggled to unravel the intricacies of the various games. I did realise I was watching something very different to what I had experienced both in my upbringing in Wales, and in my early coaching courses in England. There was little evidence of structured drills and static practices. Instead, games started in a variety of movement situations that continually seemed to change. The English boys were experiencing significant challenges in their decision-making processes. These game challenges would not have been part of their previous coaching experiences. Those game practices, I suggest, would have been much more structured.

I spoke to Pierre after the session. He arranged a visit for me to his home base of Toulouse, where he was lead coach of the Stade Toulousain team. I visited the following summer and stayed in the city for a week as a guest of Pierre. Here, I began the long journey of gaining more understanding of Pierre's coaching methods with a team that was at the highest level of the French club game.

I visited his school, Lycée Joliment. This was one of a number of schools having the status of 'centre of rugby excellence'. At this time, French rugby had many schools, mostly in the South of France, whose role was to develop the best players from the region for selection to national age group teams. The boys selected to attend the school had three afternoons of coaching with coaches of high level. Here, Pierre's philosophy had a very positive effect on the young players.

COACHING AT STADE TOULOUSAIN

After observing two coaching sessions at the Toulouse club, I began to recognise the benefits of his coaching at the elite level of the game. The skills of movement, handling and decision-making were of a standard I had not seen in British rugby. I realised these skills were not a result of 'French flair' but of a coaching method that relied heavily on strategic and tactical training.

The warm ups rarely involved the coaches. Senior players led this part of the training. Both teams of 15 played a game of semi-contact rugby at half pace. To a large extent, the game was cooperative, with defenders just blocking and holding. The defenders did not take the ball even if poorly presented. The attackers developed their understanding of how to penetrate the defence. This meant that the lines of running and the moving or fixing of defenders were very effective. Support play and realignment proved a constant challenge. The players had to ask themselves continuously, 'what is my role and positioning near and further from the ball'. In the practice of around twenty minutes, I only saw the ball dropped two or three times. Continuous game practice, in this co-operative style, allowed players the freedom to make choices both individually and collectively. The questions for the attacking players to ask were; 'Can I influence and help the ball carrier?' and 'Do I recognise where the next immediate action is likely to be?'. The players constantly encountered many game situations that required similar but not exact responses. The game's principles of 'go forward and support' underpinned the methodology. The defenders worked similarly in basic roles of defensive play regarding positioning, alignment and communication, but without taking the ball.

THE BAYEUX TAPESTRY OF RUGBY

After training one evening, Pierre invited me for dinner in a restaurant in Toulouse with the players. After dinner I asked Pierre to explain some of the ideas behind his playing philosophy. Those of you who know French restaurants will be familiar with their expansive paper table cloths. As I had no notepad, Pierre proceeded to write his coaching strategies and tactics, complete with diagrams, on an ever-increasing length of 'papier blanc'. As the evening wore on, and over an hour later, we had accumulated over 10 metres of prime tablecloth! I duly rolled up the paper cloth, stuffed it under my shirt, and took it to my hotel room to digest!! I wish I had kept this gem of a coaching manual for display in the archives of rugby coaching. C'est la vie!

As the training session developed, the emphasis was almost totally on the movement between set pieces. When they practised a lineout, sometimes it took place along the length of the field rather than the conventional side of the pitch. This was an example of Pierre's approach in constantly using innovative and challenging tactical situations. The intensity of the training increased as the session developed. If mistakes occurred, such as a spilled ball, the defence immediately counter-attacked. It was during this period, from 1981 to the late eighties, that the Toulouse style of rugby began to evolve under Pierre's tutelage. Players such as Jean-Pierre Rives,

'Why play against the wall when it is easier to go through the door'

Jean-Claude Skrela, Guy Noves (later to become the Toulouse coach and National coach), and Denis Charvet, (all French national players) began to flourish. More than half of the Toulouse team at that time were in the National side. They relished the freedom to find collective solutions to the challenges Pierre set them.

COACHING AT OXFORD UNIVERSITY

In the early nineties, Pierre came to Oxford University to assist in our preparation for the Varsity match. During a pre-season training session, run by Pierre, a perplexed South African scrum half, Micky Kirsten, asked Pierre 'What do you want me to do at the rucks?' He asked, 'Do you want me to pass, run or kick.' An amused Pierre answered – 'I don't know, you choose'. You could not blame Micky who was clearly a product of overly structured coaching.

In 1992, Pierre came to assist me in our preparations for the University game at Twickenham, I was able to see him at work with the students for many hours. He did a pre-season of a week with us and four other visits during the term. The Oxford captain David Henderson, a durable and effervescent young Scottish hooker was enthusiastic to embrace Pierre's methods.

Pierre's work focussed exclusively on game play in movement. His methods seemed to polarise players' approaches to the coaching. There were those for whom the excitement and challenge of the tactical situations presented were stimulating. Others who had experienced a more structured approach in their coaching were less effusive. Even with students at Oxford, some minds remained reluctant to experience a different challenge.

After one frustrating morning session, Pierre asked the players to go in the changing room for a brief talk. When all were seated, he asked a simple question. 'If you are going to leave the changing room how will you go out?'

A brief and eerie silence followed. Then, Patrick Coveney from Dublin, and son of the Irish deputy prime minister, and himself a future politician if ever there was, ventured, 'Pierre, I presume you mean by opening the door.' To which the reply came, 'Of course, but why on the pitch do we always play against the wall!'. This brought wry smiles all round.

I continued the work Pierre had begun, during a pre-season OURFC tour to Canada. Pierre also made some return visits. We played some exciting rugby and beat the Romania National team and several first-class teams. That team included Gareth Rees, a Canadian international who was the first player to appear in four World Cups. Our record was one of the best while I was coaching at Oxford. The team played the style of rugby that Pierre encouraged. Even so, a few key players found the freedom of choosing how to play difficult when put under pressure.

Pierre delivered a pre-game talk the night before the Varsity game. He said the big challenge was to play in the pressure of what he termed the 'big theatre'. This was when emotional elements could affect certain players in their capacity to play under pressure. Several key scoring moments in the game went unrewarded as players took poor choices of play. We narrowly lost the game.

Nevertheless, Pierre stayed for the Varsity Ball. This after -match social occasion took place on HMS Belfast, a historic warship anchored in the Thames as a museum. Pierre did not go to bed that night as, later at the hotel, he stayed up sharing stories with the players. He told me how much he enjoyed the very traditional British experience.

Following this visit, I maintained contact with Pierre. Ever since that time, I continue to look for challenges and to discover more about the rugby 'in movement'. I have attended and then assisted as coach on the Plaisir du Mouvement (PDM) courses in France. My specialism is in ball-related warm-ups, linking skills with the tactical elements of the game.

LE PLAISIR DU MOUVEMENT

For over 20 years, Pierre has led a group of like-minded French coaches and administrators who wish to preserve their philosophy of coaching rugby. This group have formed a non-profit-making company 'Le Plaisir du Mouvement' in a bid to preserve the special nature of this form of coaching, using sound educational prin-

Pierre Villepreux coaching

ciples. The philosophy is one of rugby taught at the level of tactical understanding of the majority of the players, whether they are nine or nineteen. It is certainly not about technical expertise taking precedence over understanding the tactical game.

The group organises courses run for a week. At present, they arrange three one-week courses, two held in France, and one in Treviso in Italy. I am hoping to start such a course in England in the near future.

The courses are open to players of all standards. They are not just for elite players. The courses require little advertising, as within a week of the course registration they are filled. They succeed through word of mouth about the unique content of the course, which is a thorough understanding of rugby 'in movement'. The coaches invited to attend receive no payment, apart from travel expenses. They come to further their understanding of the coaching process and to support Pierre. Many of the coaches are teachers. Most coach at age group level in some of the top clubs in France, such as Toulouse, Stade Francais and Bordeaux.

Players are grouped loosely in age bands. However, the groupings take account of their tactical understanding of the moving game. Certainly, some physically bigger players would move up an age group, as would some

STAGES
Pierre VILLEPREUX

Organisés par l'Association
Le Plaisir du Mouvement
BP 171 - 85303 CHALLANS cedex
Tél./fax : 05 61 76 54 41
Agrément FFR et Jeunesse et Sport en cours

younger players who were more tactically advanced in their game understanding. Some older players would join a lower age band, where they would find the tactical development was more appropriate. Some of the French coaches have been working on the course for twenty years. Some of the most experienced are Yannick Debaisieux from Bordeaux; Sam Lacombe, the current Toulouse U18 coach; David Hourau the Corsica Rugby Development manager; Olivier Baragnon and Jeff Beltran.

The U18 age group has the capacity both to learn and to apply the game principles, as their skill levels enable them to work effectively. I took Joe Winpenny, a 17-year-old from Oxford, to Pierre's course in the late 80s. Joe has since returned to attend the course as a coach and is the present coach of Oxford Brookes university rugby club. He is a true convert to the coaching philosophy. My grandson Rory is doing the same. He attended two Villepreux courses as a player and has since returned to experience the course from the other side, as a coach! Another grandson Cameron, has also been involved on the course as a translator, mostly for his grandfather!

In 2011, I took four players at the U15 age group from Chinnor Rugby Club to experience this 'different' coaching style. On returning they made such comments as these:

> 'The rugby was very different; the lines were so much faster than they are in England, and with no scrums or line outs, it was very much a movement game.' 'Overall it was a worthwhile experience'. 'I learned more about my strengths and areas for development, and I would say that under the English facade beats the heart of an Italian!'

Rory had been playing rugby for only 2 years.

> 'My Trip to France was an enjoyable experience. I found that the rugby in France is so different to the head down and run forward method that I use in England. The rugby was a challenge being in the U17s, but I liked the way it was just me. In the rugby we were told look for support after contact which was the opposite of what I'd been taught at Chinnor.'

Jack was 15.

In attendance at these courses were players from Morocco, Luxembourg, Holland, Italy and even as far away as Martinique. Their coaches accompanied these players and came to observe and to learn. In 2014, I took eight coaches including two high performance coaches from the RFU. Perhaps we may see some development game-centred approach in England. I continue to spread the word to encourage young British coaches to attend the French courses.

Every day Pierre held a meeting for coaches for one hour in the morning and one hour in the afternoon. At these meetings, he would discuss the methodology used in the sessions and invite questions from the group. He addressed the group in French, Italian and English! I also gave some input to the coaches, with contributions on how we could more closely link relevant skills to the game. I outlined how we might develop more ball skills in our warm up activities through the use of games.

The players did two practical sessions a day, one in the morning and one in late afternoon. A compulsory rest period during the early afternoon ensured that the boys were fresh for the later session. A late afternoon recreational time enabled the players to indulge in non-rugby activities led by French PE students. Evenings provided down-time or activities organised by the PE students supervising the players. The course also enabled English speaking players to improve their 'French language' skills. This enabled an educational input from the course. We had to justify them having a week off school!

When I worked for the RFU as a Development Officer, Pierre and I arranged a sharing of coaching knowledge between the development officers in France and, in our case, the Southern Region Rugby Development Officers. These annual exchanges enabled both countries to share their expertise in the coaching methods. The English side provided a more technical offering and the French the game-centred approach. The annual exchanges coincided with the France v England Six Nations game. These events proved beneficial to both sides. As the connections became established, leading French coaches, such as Didier Retiere, who became a National coach presented on regional courses in the UK. I took a number of our leading coaches to present on the technical merits of set piece play to invited French coaches. I still think there is merit in continuing this sort of work. The Villepreux rugby culture has differences with the traditional coaching philosophy. Both countries would benefit from sharing ideas in the content and methodology of coaching.

Pierre began his teaching career in Toulouse, where he played for the Stade team. Soon he was appointed Head of the Physical Education National rugby programme at Lycée Joliment in the city. Here, the most talented boys at U15 age group in the region gained selection to the school of excellence, one of more than fifteen spread throughout the country. France, at this time, was ahead of other countries in the development programme for recognising and nourishing young talented players. The coaches, all rugby playing PE teachers, were the best of those graduating from the universities. For Pierre, this was a chance to work with boys for up to ten hours a week putting his coaching beliefs to work. As he finished playing, he continued this work. He began to see how, by introducing players to these coaching methods, they were becoming freer to express themselves in the game. The experience of constantly changing tactical decisions, through the medium of game play, was a major reason why players were graduating to high level French clubs (many to Toulouse) and soon into the National team. In the late eighties, the French squad of thirty players on tour to New Zealand contained the remarkable number of sixteen players who had graduated from Joliment. Maybe, the French should not have abandoned this effective production line where trained teachers coached the boys.

Pierre's engaging personality and his capacity to share his knowledge with others were great assets. The French government asked him to introduce rugby to their former colony, Tahiti. This was a great opportunity for Pierre to test his theories in a country where rugby had never been played. What an amazing three-year programme transpired. As an introduction to the complex game of rugby, the first sessions involved a game that was essentially rugby without the set pieces. He decided to begin with no skills training, just a reasonable space to play. At first, games were one v one and soon graduated to team play of up to ten v ten. He ensured that games followed basic rules of rugby such as tackling, release of the ball in tackle and offside. He used basic understandable language to assist the players. Such phrases as 'Go forward', 'Go help him', 'Look for another', were all they required. He has done similar projects in other countries. All of his coaching follows the principles he employed in Tahiti.

The principles apply as much to elite players as to beginners. The difference is only one of experience and increased competence in skills and exposure to the coaching methods. More recently, he led a project in another former French colony, Madagascar, over a period of a few days, and achieved exactly the same results. These boys were from poor areas and had not experienced or seen rugby. Yet they were achieving great things within a short time. Pierre used the phrase to me, 'They were incredible'.

In his capacity as Head Coach of Toulouse, in the late seventies and eighties, he transformed an underachieving major club into one of the most exciting teams in Europe. I was fortunate to observe in some detail his coaching methods, during the week I visited Toulouse. I watched all the training sessions, including some age-group coaching sessions. I spent further time with Pierre as he explained in more detail the theory behind the coaching process. As a consequence, my coaching philosophy changed.

Toulouse dominated European rugby during his time at the club. Toulouse gained a favourable reputation because they played, as some journalists said, 'With style and panache'.

As with many things in French rugby, politics play a disproportionate part in its development. The French President appoints the National coach. For the period in preparation for the 1999 World Cup, the President appointed Jean-Claude Skrela, who was Pierre's assistant at Toulouse. Pierre and the President were not exactly on friendly terms. Fortunately, Skrela was shrewd enough to realise that he could appoint his own assistant coaches. As he was basically the forwards coach, he asked Pierre to join him. The journey of the French team to the World Cup was interesting. The team won back to back grand slams, winning the Six Nations by playing some inspired rugby. Pierre knew that gelling the team to play the rugby he wanted them to play was not easy. Differing playing styles in the club teams meant the National team found it hard to play consistently in the way Pierre and Jean-Claude wanted. In the qualifying rounds, France struggled to win matches. The team only just scraped through to the quarter finals. They improved enough to reach the semi-finals only to be rewarded with a game against the almighty, all-conquering All Blacks!

What turned out at Twickenham, on that Sunday afternoon in 1999, was one of the most remarkable games ever played in a World Cup. I was fortunate to be at the game with my wife, Mary. The first half saw the New Zealand team dominate possession. They played with a confidence gained from winning their previous matches in convincing style and scoring freely. Early on in the game, the legendary Jonah Lomu brushed aside would-be defenders to power over for a try. New Zealand were dominant. They went in at half-time with a comfortable lead. France could never come back!

I take up the story in Lubersac, during one of Pierre's coaching courses. I asked him what happened at half-time during that game and what did he say to the team. He had noticed the space behind the All Blacks' defence was sparse and not always covering the areas. He saw that Jonah was not so agile when turning to chase kicks. He told the French forwards to play their close, short passing game to drag in the defence to create space for the backs. A transformation took place immediately after half-time. Lamaisson the fly half dropped a goal, He continued to use the kicking game to exploit spaces behind the defence. One of these kicks resulted in a try. As the confidence flowed into the French team, conversely it seemed to ebb from the All Blacks. The French team began to play as they had trained. Their now power-driven pack of forwards produced quick ball. The consummate skills of the backs opened up spaces in the demoralised and somewhat disorganised New Zealand defence. France had performed a rugby miracle in the space of forty minutes. Pierre's reading of the game and his persuasion of the French players to believe in the 'game' they had trained to play enabled the team to turn the game around. This was not an easy task because the mental toughness of French players is often questioned. This game was to be their World Cup pinnacle. They lost the final, in Cardiff, to Australia. Pierre believes the publicity and media attention on the players while they prepared proved to be a huge distraction. Situated in the centre of the capital city of Wales was in stark contrast to their base for the pool stages in the vibrant metropolis of urban Slough.

Pierre went on to head up the French Federation's national coaching programme. Despite rewriting the syllabus for the coaching processes to be rolled out across France, it seemed many French coaches were reluctant to adapt this more tactically based coaching and persisted with the more structured methods. The French decline in their position in world rugby could in some ways be attributed to not adopting a coaching method that suited French culture. The present Toulouse teams have restructured their game under former player Emile N'tmack, and the 'we see the game' in France begin to flourish again.

Pierre and I continue to exchange and develop ideas to enhance our coaching. I am using more skill-related practices in warm-ups. The slogan 'A Ball for All' is one I would like to see used more in schools and clubs, to enable players to improve their skills. In addition, we are looking at the inclusion of a tactical 'games' element into these skills, to help players link more closely to the game. Pierre has and continues to have a huge influence on my coaching.

LITTLEMORE RFC

The 'safety first' concept is still strong in the philosophy of coaches. Perhaps the coach needs to know the player well and read what he does. Near the game practices develop this understanding.'

Kevin Bowring – Wales Coach and RFU Elite Development Coach

During the early 1970s, education in Oxford City underwent radical change. This change introduced a new arrangement for schools. A three-tier school organisation replaced the primary to secondary system. Pupils aged 5 to 9 attended First Schools; those aged 9 to 13 went to Middle Schools and youngsters aged 13 to 18 entered Upper Schools. Introducing rugby to boys as old as eleven had proved challenging in the past. The new school system of introducing rugby to boys aged thirteen proved even more difficult. Year by year, the standard of schoolboy rugby was declining. Rugby in state schools suffered from having fewer teachers volunteering to take after-school clubs. This was, in large part, a result of many teachers' angry reaction to government policies regarding school activities. Few of our rugby playing leavers joined local clubs. Most of our intake came from two of the largest housing estates. These boys did not feel comfortable going into 'foreign' areas of the city.

In 1976, I and the Community Lead Officer, a Scotsman, Alan Noble, invited people in Littlemore to an open meeting to consider the future of rugby in the area. Over twenty people attended. This meeting resulted in the birth of Littlemore Rugby Club. Over half the group were former pupils and others were newcomers to rugby or people new to the area. I felt it was vital to provide opportunities for the local community to play rugby. The head of the school, the visionary Bob Moon, formerly a successful head of a thriving community school in Milton Keynes, was hugely supportive. He offered the school's playing facilities, free of charge, for the new club to train and play. A local hotelier running the George Hotel in the village, Jim Adams, cheerfully hosted the club for post-match meals and refreshments. He realised a surge in profits could result, as a host of rugby players not noted for being abstemious, sampled his very decent ales. He was very welcoming and supportive of the whole club.

A rugby mad, Irish pairing of the Heffernan family became important founders. They assumed administrative roles alongside Ted Brocklesby, a former Littlemore councillor and avid rugby fan. I had very recently bought Ted's spacious house situated on the perimeter of the village of Littlemore. The house was appropriately named Ty Gwyn, Welsh for 'White House'. The club elected Ted as its first president. A good friend of mine, a headteacher and convert to rugby, John Batey, provided both wisdom and vision to the new club. From the modest beginning of playing High Wycombe 7th team away, the club made good progress. Littlemore RFC became a truly community rugby team. Within ten years the club established a very competitive fixture list.

The school, via the generosity of the local educational authority, gifted a redundant classroom for a clubhouse. The members of the club refurbished the classroom.

Littlemore Rugby Football Club

LITTLEMORE RFC

–v–

PRESIDENT'S SELECT XV

19 85

Founded 1976

ON THE OCCASION OF THE
OFFICIAL OPENING OF
THEIR CLUBHOUSE
17 NOVEMBER 1985

Littlemore RFC celebrated the opening of their new club house with a game against the Kew Occasionals. It was a long night!

The work of volunteers, under the direction of Cameron Wilson, whose son Stuart played for the club, ensured the opening of the clubhouse within eighteen months.

I was an occasional player (not that my wife knew or approved). My boots were always ready in the back of my car. My role was more of a non-tackler, talking the young squad through tactics, and perfecting my dummy scissors. The side developed well. The players were strong performers in the newly created County Cup competition. On several occasions, they caused major upsets in the County Cup. The team defeated the two leading club sides, Oxford and Henley, and a very strong RAF Brize Norton team. The result of the RAF game led to a typically amusing comment from the renowned after-dinner speaker and former Scottish international, Joe McPartlin. In reply to Mr. Heffernan senior, who commented 'What a great victory', Joe responded, 'I think you should refer it to the Pope in order for him to declare it a miracle!'

One of the club's former school players was Peter Jones, a talented ball-playing hooker. Peter was rugby mad. He had the ability to play at a higher level. In his youth, his social life occasionally led him into some issues with the law. We managed to get him a trial with Bath RFC. He became understudy to England hooker Graham Dawe. Sadly, despite playing some games for Bath and impressing that club with his play, Peter found the travelling from Oxford and the discipline of attending all training too much of a hardship. He returned to play at Littlemore with his friends. He also played for OURFC in the Toulouse centenary tournament in 1990, against Paul Sabatier University. This was a huge tournament in Toulouse. Club and country sides from all over the world participated, including Fiji, Samoa, and leading New Zealand sides. Our OURFC team flew in on a private flight, laid on for us from Luton airport. We were short of a hooker. Peter played and did credit to himself with an excellent game. It made me realise how our game at the top-level favours those from a more privileged background. Their schooling and training enable them to be comfortable in such elite surroundings.

Littlemore RFC established good playing links with Oxford Polytechnic. Several talented students played in the Littlemore colours. The club arranged tours and, every Easter, Littlemore travelled to such delightful areas as Devon, Cornwall,

Littlemore Rugby Club Easter tour to Devon with a certain culinary theme!

Jersey and Cork. My roles changed. I led the team in choral renditions and was the judge in the touring assizes. My friend, John Batey, a former police officer and master of the language of the judiciary, conducted many hilarious court sessions on tour.

The competitive nature of rugby's league structures provided a big challenge for the club in recent years. Nevertheless, it is surviving and has excellent clubhouse facilities with many local groups basing their activities at the club. If the Littlemore Academy (formerly Peers School) played more rugby, I am sure students would gravitate to the club to continue playing rugby.

A YEAR OF
LABAN MODERN EDUCATIONAL DANCE

During 1971, I began a year's secondment at the Laban Art of Movement Studio in Weybridge, Surrey. Little did I realise that this 'Year of Dance' would have such an influence on some aspects of my coaching.

I realised that modern educational dance (MED) would have a big influence on my playing and coaching career. During an enlightened period in education, in the '70s, teachers received much encouragement to gain additional qualifications. Very few men took up MED courses, unsurprisingly, as prejudices were common. Comments frequently associated dance with feminine traits. Nevertheless, six males of

Rudolphe Laban Dance Innovator

mature years arrived in Weybridge, in September 1971. We joined with three times as many mature women, to study a year's course in Rudolf Laban's modern dance.

This dance course had an unexpectedly important influence on my thinking about the physical and mental preparation for a physical game like rugby. I did not fully appreciate this influence, until many years after I had completed the course. In our first practical dance session, at the studio, all the males wore rugby shirts and shorts. By necessity, we were in bare feet. Within a week, we wore the same attire as the women, namely, leotards and tights. These were much more pragmatic for movement!

All of the women had experience in dance, whereas none of the men had any previous, relevant experience. We were mostly intent on gaining a qualification enabling us to become lecturers in teacher training colleges. Rudolf Laban was a dance teacher of Hungarian descent. He had a major influence on the method of teaching dance. He began working in Europe in 1930. His co-teacher, Lisa Ullman, continued Laban's dance legacy and his theories had a major influence on the teaching of modern dance. At the time I attended the studio, she was the principal. The Laban movement has expanded and encompasses a large gathering of dedicated academics in the fields of music, dance, drama and associated disciplines.

Our work at the studio, set in idyllic surroundings, was a combination of inventive movement, drama and notation of the dance process. Laban's theory examines the many methods by which the body can move most efficiently in time and space. The dance encourages individuals to express their creativity and emotions through body movement.

The principles of the Laban Dance are not easy to explain in a few paragraphs. Nevertheless, I will attempt to explain how they impacted on me.

The dance training made me aware of the personal space in which I move parts of my body, which does not change. Then, I needed to explore the space beyond that, into which I can move, that constantly changes. The qualities of the movements that emanate to and from the body's centre, are complex and varied. For example, the direction of movements can be direct or flexible, or a combination of both. The speed of the movement can be faster or slower. The movement can flow or be stilted. The movement can be strong or very light. These qualities of movement can also occur within the same movement pattern. For example, a movement can begin with force and speed, and fade into lightness with less speed. In rugby, as in most sports, such movements are frequent. A player off-loading a delicate short pass with one hand, could, with the other hand use a strong, fending movement to hold off a defender. When disguising a type of pass, by winding up the arms to deliver a long fast pass, a player could take the power from the pass by slowing and releasing the energy, to give a short pop pass. My training, in the Laban system, made me more aware of how I could control my body.

When movements occur in the 360 degrees around your body, the training makes you more aware of the movements in your 'personal space'. Training to use appropriate movements in the whole range from low to medium to high, is applicable to all areas in rugby. An additional need is training to move rhythmically with control and imagination. In response to encouragement, we invented our own dance, sometimes to music or other stimuli, such as clapping, humming, tapping, chanting. Another important aspect of our training encouraged us to create dances as individuals, pairs, small or large groups. In the initial stages, such creativity was quite challenging for the men, as we had little experience. As the course progressed, the men brought a different dynamism to the dance. This required lifting and other powerful movements to combine with the more refined movements necessary for contrast. As an all-male dance group, we did a public performance, dancing to the rhythms of the Burundi Black drums. That was one of the most demanding, physical, emotional, and stimulating experiences in my life.

In terms of body conditioning, I was never as 'all round fit'. My agility improved and my endurance base increased. I became more flexible and, above all, more aware of what was happening in the space all around me. Every morning, our mature student group had an hour's work on flexibility exercises and rhythmic movements. Our general movement increased awareness of where, when, how and why our bodies moved more effectively and efficiently. On one occasion, a couple of members of the Ballet Rambert Dance Group visited. They took us through a typical warm up, used before their dance training class began. The session took an hour and a half. I could hardly move the next day. We made frequent visits to the Palace Theatre in London, where dance productions using Laban's methods took place.

Our dance group had a weekly session observing and discussing efficient movement in general life and, especially, in the workplace. Our tutor once took us to a coffee shop to watch several people at work. We were to observe the staff to see who worked with the least amount of effort and in the quickest time. We then had to discuss what movements made the work of the most efficient staff different from the others. I believe that, in a game of rugby, we can become more fluent, through greater awareness of our bodies. We need to experience more training of the body that matches the needs of the individual. Training should not be so generalised, as that I see in most warm ups. I have tried to incorporate some of the movements involved in warm ups with some of the movement choices in Laban Dance. Rhythmic movements, in general, help the body to stay more in balance. This is an important quality to have on a rugby field. In rugby, particularly in contact situations, it is necessary, when in possession of the ball, to have part of the body tense and strong while another part has less tension and greater control in the movement. Those movements are the basis of Laban Dance. Efficient and trained movements can certainly help to avoid injury. Too often, warm-up movements are stylised and rigid. The dance-trained person moves to and from his/her central core in the most effective ways. By encouraging the players to explore the range of possibilities in movement, we need to engage them in a less mechanical way. A former pupil of mine, Anne Wheeler who swam competitively for Wales and Great Britain, later became a teacher of Pilates and Laban Dance. One of my aims is to get her to conduct a warm up session with a group of rugby players. One of her students is none other than the Queen of Norway.

Rugby is becoming more physical as the players become bigger and more powerful. The speed of the game has increased. There is a requirement for us all to examine how we can improve the way we move in the game. With rugby facing increased scrutiny regarding safety for players, there appears to be a good case for inclusion of this type of dance training.

I want to convey the value I gained through the awareness of the space and movement of players that I experienced in my dance training. I seemed to 'see' many more things happening simultaneously. During my year of dance training I became more aware of actions occurring both close to my position and in the wider parts of the pitch. It was almost as if I was watching the game from above the playing area.

OXFORD UNIVERSITY RFC

'Don't spend time beating on a wall, hoping to transform it into a door.'
Coco Chanel – Actress

The Oxford University Rugby Club (OURFC) did not wholly embrace the role of coaching. Many of its former players served on the committee of the Rugby Football Union, who were custodians of the amateur game. The archdeacon of amateurism, Dudley Wood, was an alumnus of Oxford. Dudley was an outstanding administrator. He strongly supported the view of rugby remaining as an amateur game.

In 1980, I received a phone call from the secretary of OURFC, Simon Halliday, the future Bath and England centre. Someone had forwarded my name to OURFC as a possible coach to the rugby club. After a meeting with Simon and the captain Nigel Roberts, an undergraduate and very personable member of Jesus College, I accepted the generous offer. In the wording of the official letter confirming my appointment, my role was 'to assist the Captain in the preparation of the team for

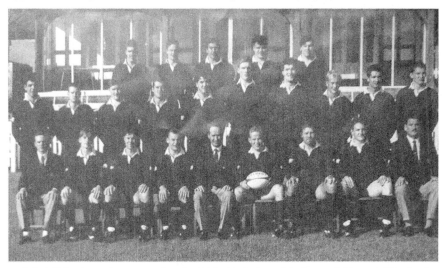

Oxford University touring group to Canada 1993 taken in front of the famous clubhouse at Iffley Road

the Varsity Match'! There was to be no payment, just the privilege of coaching a university team with a rich rugby history.

The crowded fixture list playing first class clubs during the term of the Varsity match put huge pressure on the relatively small playing squad. The team played as many as eight fixtures against some of the leading clubs in the British game. The forwards, especially, faced tough, physical challenges as they encountered wizened and hardened forwards three times in eight days. A typical example would be Blackheath, followed by Cardiff (always away) and finishing with Gloucester. Today, Oxford's fixture list cannot feature games against full-time professional sides, as the gulf in standards is far too wide.

From a coaching and playing perspective, games against the international teams were particularly special occasions. International teams in those days made lengthy tours of the U.K. They considered a fixture with OURFC as useful for the warm-up stages of these tours. During my tenure as coach, we played Tonga, Western Samoa (Samoa now), Romania, Canada and Australia. We did well to win two of these matches. The opportunity to prepare and play against these national teams provided valuable experiences both for players and coaches. Attention to detail in our preparation became more important. I frequently asked specialist coaches with more detailed knowledge of the set pieces, to pass on their expertise to forwards.

During my early period of coaching at Oxford, our arch-opponents, Cambridge, had a more effective process of attracting post-graduate students. Their main post-graduate course, Land Economy, (the syllabus of this course remained a mystery to me) was a two-year course, while Oxford's main attraction was the one-year diploma in Sociology commonly known as the Dip Soc. Keeping students for two years was a huge advantage. Cambridge won most of the games in the early eighties. By the late eighties, Oxford had improved their recruitment programme by asking former players from around the world, to encourage students to apply for the two-year courses. Coupled to this, a range of scholarships was available and a few admissions tutors in the colleges had an empathy with rugby. At this time in 1986, a close friend of mine, Simon Winman, an avid admirer of the game-based approach, started coaching the U21 team. This meant that some of the outstanding undergraduates, maturing into the Blues squad, had previous experience of this coaching approach.

The coaching challenge at Oxford and Cambridge was to find methods of playing that would counteract the maturity, especially in forward play, when we played against the strong first-class club teams. Without exception, clubs would try and dominate the forward game, using their superior physical skills. This limited the students' quality and quantity of possession from the set pieces. Our approach was to speed up our game to ensure longer periods of continuous play. The aim was to tire the less fit club forwards. The problem for me was that very few of our players were familiar with the game-based approach. The coaching they would have received would have been very structured with excessive emphasis on unit play (backs and forwards working apart). Frequently, I had to adjust my coaching style to ensure the team were comfortable with a balance between the structured and the game-based approaches. Some of the players were more highly skilled and motivated to a risk-taking approach. Less skilled players would generally feel less confident in the game-based style. In conjunction with the captain, we would decide where to prioritise the balance in our coaching. The 1988 team was exceptional. These players had both the ability to play well and willingness to try different approaches. I would spend most of my time, when coaching back play, to begin practices from more random positions. I tried to get away from the more ordered, linear attacking. I would give it the term, 'disorder to order'. I wanted to encourage the team to play against varying forms of defence, for example, grouped, spread, deep and close. In this way, decision-making opportunities put players under greater scrutiny and pressure. In this method of coaching, the players experience a myriad of tactical situations, to which they need to find the better solutions. We tried to perfect our set moves that operated as close to the defensive line as possible. These moves required to be practised as close to the pressure experienced in the game, with the necessary skill and timing. We worked in conjunction with the back row, when the flankers were not required for set piece work. In most line out practices I observed the open side flanker was mostly a spectator. The 88 team was capable of pulling many top clubs' defences apart from a set play. By practising against a live defence, players' decisions were closer to those of a real game.

For the physical challenge facing us in most matches, we needed to tackle well. We had to negate the close contact, driving game designed to take energy from our game. Wet conditions always provided the hardest test. Most sessions started with a series of handling exercises designed to ensure our handling game would stand up to the severest pressure. These practices would include all the players, not just the backs. Contact work on our feet was a priority, as we felt we would have a greater number of options from a maul. We relied heavily on the older, more experienced post graduate players. The range of experience in the 1981 team was wide. Among the very experienced players was an ex-England international wing and future member of parliament, Derek Wyatt. He had the reputation, while at Oxford, of never making a tackle, but making a record number of interceptions. Another player with valuable experience was a Welsh schoolboy international, Stuart Barnes, destined to play his senior rugby for England. Simon Halliday, a Canadian winger Andrew Bibby, and the ubiquitous No.8 Martin Gargan, a medic at the university, were other very capable and experienced members, who enjoyed the creative style of rugby! The rest of the team included players who had represented U18 group International sides, such as Tony Brooks a skilful No.8 and Chris Millichip a centre, or representatives of County age group teams. The challenge, as always for a Varsity game, was, within the short period of around ten weeks, to prepare the side to win

1872

1981

The 100th Varsity Match

The Presidents and Committees of the University Rugby Clubs
request the pleasure of the company of

L. Evans and guest

at the Match and for Luncheon
at Twickenham on Tuesday December 8th 1981.

12.45 for 1.00 p.m.   RSVP Dr. A.B. Tayler, St. Catherine's College, Oxford

Celebration ticket for the 100th Varsity match

that match. I used the knowledge I had acquired in Toulouse from Pierre Villepreux
to coach the style of play I believed in.

My first Varsity game just happened to coincide with the staging of the 100th
game between Oxford and Cambridge. It was the only Varsity game played on a
pitch covered in several inches of snow. Oxford lost a strange game. The conditions
nullified the preparations and plans of both teams. Cambridge edged the result 9 –
6. The evening's celebrations were quite special with royalty in attendance in the
presence of Prince Andrew.

Many of the players, especially the more experienced ones, who had learned to
play in structured ways, found it difficult to adapt to the game style of play. They felt
uncomfortable when coaching required them to take more of their own decisions. I
was beginning to understand the challenges I was facing with this more player-centred coaching. Players used to being directed by the coach become very conditioned
to the more structured coaching style. The longer period they have been coached
in structure, the more challenging it is for them to accept more ownership of their
decision making in less structured situations.

Frequently, during my time at Oxford, I invited coaches whom I knew would add
some gravitas to our game. These coaches included Chalky White (Leicester and
RFU), Alan Davies (Nottingham and Wales) and, in one season, Pierre Villepreux
(Toulouse and France). The obvious objective of coaching Oxford and Cambridge
Universities is to win the annual Varsity match. The result of the Varsity game

defined their season. It was difficult for me to achieve my broader aim of changing the playing style, in what was essentially a ten-week season of high-pressure games.

The role of university captain entitled them to invite coaches they knew and had previously worked with at their previous university. Most captains consulted with me before such an arrangement was made. A few did not. These coaches normally arrived around three weeks before the game. Two such captains of OURFC had been coached by Alan Jones, coach to Australia at the time, and Alan Solomons coach at Cape Town university, and later South African coach, and coach to a number of professional clubs in England. Much of what they did was to do with game structure and organisation.

I did not think that it was always wise to bring in someone, however talented a coach, at a late time because it resulted in players dealing with new ideas and methods. Then they had to activate these changes under the pressure of the Varsity match. As my role was to support the captain, this system proved to be very challenging for me. Some captains wanted to play a more structured game that was in conflict with the other coaching they received. On only one occasion did Oxford win the Varsity game in the years when the guest coach came. The captains who trusted my coaching methods most believed the team could succeed in playing this style of game. They supported the method by using their close support group of players within the team. We have to remember that the roles of captain at both Oxford and Cambridge remained true to the amateur ethos of captaincy. Coaching was just there to assist in the team's preparation. How individual captains interpreted this depended on their trust in me as the coach.

Within three weeks of the Varsity term in 1981 we had our first major test. We played Australia at Iffley Road. The tourists of the UK in those days usually had, in theory at least, more winnable fixtures to start the tour. That day, Oxford surpassed themselves, losing by only 11 – 19 to an Australian team containing the three Ella brothers, among the most gifted players to represent their country. They played rugby that reflected the indigenous nature of players brought up in an environment free from structure. It helped in our preparation that Phil Crowe, a post-graduate recently arrived from Sydney, had played for Australia the year before. We knew most of their plays. Wyatt had his speciality interception try. Stuart Barnes showed what a talent he was going to be. He thrived on competition. Stuart came to Oxford as a schoolboy international full back, with great pace, vision and buckets of self-belief. We asked him if he would play at fly-half, 'Of course I can play there' came the confident reply.

The night of the Varsity game saw four inches of snow fall on Twickenham. The game could not be postponed as the Varsity Game was celebrating its centenary match with royalty in attendance. We lost the Varsity game, played in the freak, snowy conditions 6 – 9, all kicks. For Cambridge, Rob Andrew was one of three freshmen destined to play for England. He was a lifetime challenger for the England number 10 jersey with Stuart. If ever there was a greater contrast in playing styles this was it. England settled mostly for the more conservative and structured approach. The Varsity game in those days was almost like a further England trial match.

As a coach, I was beginning to realise the huge importance to the players and universities of winning the Varsity game. In many ways, I appreciated what each captain's main objective was. I also felt there was a bigger picture for the Universities to consider. The quality of some of the Varsity games in the seventies was very poor, with periods of handling rugby noticeable by their absence. This style of rugby would not attract more spectators to watch this pre-Christmas showpiece. Attendances began to decline. So would sponsorship, if dire matches were to become the norm. We were one of the first university teams to establish pre-season fitness tests, courtesy of the sister University at Oxford Brookes. Many of these were laboratory-based tests. VO2 testing on a treadmill was a relatively new test for club-based teams. Fat calliper testing of body fat and strength testing were pre-season activities. Attendances at Twickenham began to rise in the 80s. Over 60,000 attended the 1988 game. As we know, professional rugby and the rise of autumn international fixtures at Twickenham, have had an adverse effect on the attendances at the Varsity game. I hope that if the teams continue to play with vision and innovation, the historic game will survive.

I enhanced my coaching experiences through pre-season tours to many countries, including Hong Kong, Taiwan, Japan, Italy, France, Ireland and Canada. I saw the differing playing styles of the time. I admired the clockwork precision of the Japanese with their fast and accurate handling but noticed their inability to improvise. In Ireland, I saw the rugged forward game and kicking game that ensured the ball was in the air for much of the time. In Canada, physical confrontation was the prime route to go forward. In France, the passionate atmosphere in Perpignan and the dubious combative events of early forward exchanges were a delight for the crowd. Every country in which we toured gave the University a special welcome. The name of Oxford is well known across the world. Our hosts treated us as honoured guests. The Italians, during the period of the early nineties, possessed a number of gifted players with high skills. However, the lack of coaches of quality hindered their development. The Italian Federation needed to fast track promising coaches to raise levels of playing. Football is much further ahead as the National game. The playing of rugby, by and large, mainly occurs in a swathe from Venice to Rovigo in the north of the country.

I achieved my greatest ambition as a choir master in the ancient outdoor theatre in Verona. The team was on a tour of the outdoor arena. A number of us had gathered in the centre of the arena. It was the performance stage. They encouraged me to conduct a song. I can still remember the passionate rendering of the Welsh Hymn,

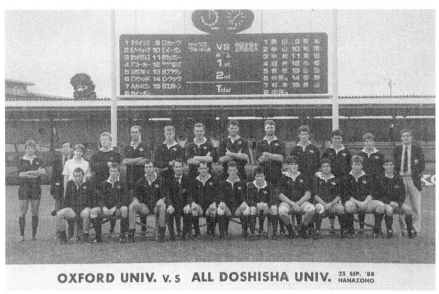

OXFORD UNIV. v. s ALL DOSHISHA UNIV. 25 SEP. '88 HANAZONO

The tours to Japan were always special and the attendances at games numbers many thousands

Cwm Rhondda to this day. The many tourists in the theatre applauded our efforts.

Japan was special. Oxford University was the first rugby team to visit Japan after the end of World War Two. This happened in 1952 under the captaincy of Giles Bullard, later Sir Giles. Japan Rugby never forgot this generous gesture. During

Special blazer badge for the 88 tour. This team was one of Oxford's best ever.

my time as coach, we visited the country on three occasions. Our hosts met all expenses. Japanese crowds in excess of thirty thousand were common in our matches. David Kirk, New Zealand and captain of his country at the first Rugby World Cup in 1987, was in our party in 1988. People mobbed him like a pop star, wherever he went.

It was in Japan that my strengths as a choir master came to the fore. I was grateful for studying choral singing while at St. Luke's College. I am certain that we made many friends with the Japanese as we shared our harmonies with the opposition and the many supporters. I continued to do this throughout my career both as a player and a coach. Singing is a wonderful way to bring groups together to share the pleasure that harmonious singing brings. Not a dirty ditty in sight and no shouting aloud. My Welsh upbringing in the land of male voice choirs made its mark with me. Some might say I was a better conductor than a rugby coach!

OURFC celebrate a win on an Irish tour against University of Cork played on a rather muddy pitch.

I worked with some of the finest rugby players both in the UK and in the major rugby playing nations of New Zealand, Australia and South Africa. Among the alumni were Irish internationals Hugo MacNeill, Brendan Mullin, and David Humphreys. All made significant contributions to Oxford rugby. Hugo became captain, while David won his first Irish cap after an astonishing display as fly-half in the Varsity game. I have rarely seen a more consuming all-round game, both as an individual player and tactical director, than David's.

The Australians, Rob Egerton and Brendan Nasser, Phil Crowe and Ian Williams, Rugby World Cup winners with Australia in the 1991 final in Twickenham, were outstanding young men. They were also special players in their own way; Rob with his alternative game as a full back and Brendan with his smiling, uncompromising style of play. Brendan had vast Test match experience and knew all the short cuts around the field. He had the ability to lead the forwards and encouraged the younger players in some of the stressful forward combats. Brendan was not the most fastidious of trainers as the ravages of Test Match rugby had resulted in deterioration of his knees. He led the forward coaching skills. The forwards respected him highly, as his knowledge of the finer parts of forward play and the dark arts, was immense. He was also a great team player with an understated style of humour. Ian Williams possessed electric pace and scored many tries from his own half of the field.

South Africans were mostly representatives of their Provincial teams. Fanie de Toit, a delightful and clever scrum half, was a product of the famous Stellenbosch University, and had come under the influence of the legendary South African coach and mentor, Danie Craven. Malcolm Brown, a centre with immaculate passing skills and a product of the University of Cape Town, was an astute reader of the game. A challenge for coaching was trying to integrate the developing skills of the undergraduates with the more mature game of the postgraduate players. I continued the work on individual skills that I had introduced with the boys at Littlemore Grammar School. Players at all levels still need to hone and improve their positional skills. The half backs, being the link between forwards and backs, need to be very precise and accurate with their passing and kicking game. They perform these skills more than any other players in the side. I would often invite seasoned scrum halves to the school to work on techniques and reaction skills under pressure. Andy Moore, a future Welsh scrum half, Steve Pearson, the present Club RFU representative and Fanie du Toit were particularly conscientious, persistent and hard working. The scrum halves frequently came to the gymnasium at my school, where we worked on the finer details of improving their technical skills. To give an example of the quality and humanity of the players at Oxford, I mention Fanie, who went on to be a member of Nelson Mandela's Reconciliation Group, who were charged with trying to reunite the post-apartheid South Africa.

One of the most successful teams of recent times was the 1988 team. That team included twelve post graduate students, six of whom were either current or future internationals. The back line was probably the best attacking unit in England at the time. These players looked to expand their game and use their skills and speed to offset the physical challenges posed by the heavier club sides. The three-quarter line included the two exciting Australians, Ian Williams and magician Rob Egerton, half backs David Kirk, hugely influential with his game knowledge and leadership, and Brian Smith, superbly skilled, David Evans the twinkle-toed, very cheeky, Cardiff centre and Malcolm Brown. David Kirk used the narrow side to attack from scrum or rucks, especially with Ian Williams on the right wing being a sprinter who could finish off most half-chances. David Evans read the game so well and would open space for support players with his evasive running. The key to that team's success, I believe, was the trust between me and the captain, Rupert Vessey, an undergraduate, an outstanding organiser and leader. We were always in conversation about how we could maximise the coaching support. I acquired the expertise of two former colleagues from St Luke's College, Andy Johnson and Dick Tilley. Both were forward specialists and helped to coach the scrum and the lineout. Senior players such as Alec Cameron, the team secretary and former Sydney University player, and David Kirk, were hugely supportive of Rupert and me. They could play! I also introduced a couple of specialist coaching sessions with Chalky White, who understood the challenges of preparation for a specific match. Some of the back play produced during the season was of such accuracy and invention that the movement and passing

A mixed OURFC team rowed the relay rugby ball for the 1991 World Cup down the river Cherwell in Oxford

skills of the backs opened up gaps virtually on top of the defence line. That season has stood out in my memory as the most rewarding of my coaching career.

I had introduced an indoor analysis session, preceding the first coaching session after a game. I would put my own analysis on a flip chart prior to the session and cover it up. Each player would then give one positive comment and another comment on how we might improve. The results were very interesting. Some of the more incisive comments came from the younger players. I think this was because they were more curious about what we could achieve. They would suggest more ambitious and less prescriptive possibilities. One young second row forward, a Welshman Simon Wensley, always looked at how we played in relationship to our strategy and the tactics we employed. Did we deviate from the way we wanted to play? David Kirk referred constantly to accuracy, or lack of it in our game. He stressed how important it was to play how we trained. The comments of the players, both positive and negative ones, were almost a match of the ones I had pre-prepared. It taught me a great lesson in looking to adopt a more player-centred approach to coaching.

In the early eighties, a powerful Australian post-graduate arrived in Oxford. He was a prop forward. He turned out to be a strong scrummager. His ball handling skills were, on the other hand, rather modest for an Australian. We had another more skilful prop available but not as effective in the scrum. Come Varsity time we had to choose one of these props. We did not select the Australian. He was particularly upset and stormed off to join the Boxing Club, though he had never boxed before. He became a hero in the University Boxing tournament, held at the Town Hall in Oxford. He stopped his Cambridge opposite number within two minutes of the bout starting, with a barrage of punches. The Cambridge trainer threw in the white towel. His bout was the decisive contest that won Oxford the match. That prop/boxer was to become Prime Minister of Australia, Tony Abbott. I invited him to speak at the annual Littlemore RFC dinner, where he gave his first 'major' public speech. He was, unsurprisingly, a very entertaining and erudite speaker.

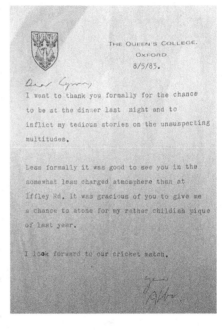

Nigel Roberts, the captain who had invited me to be the coach at Oxford, had an interesting period relating to his academic life and his future employment. He managed to attend none of his weekly tutorials at Oxford during the preparation for the Varsity match. The minimum attendance necessary to maintain residence was at least to show up occasionally. Accordingly, the University asked him to leave following the Varsity game. Within weeks, he had received offers of employment in the city, one of which he accepted. Is a degree or is captaincy of OURFC the best possible route to future employment? Discuss.

In 1993, David Henderson, a hooker and a shrewd Scot, was the elected captain of OURFC. I had spoken with David about involving Pierre Villepreux in our preparation for the game against Cambridge. He was both excited and open to having the Toulouse coach help in our preparations. Pierre attended the pre-season coaching week, before the squad set off for a tour of Canada. Our fly half Gareth Rees came from British Columbia and was the Canadian fly half at the first four World Cups.

The pre-season was most revealing. Pierre began to identify the overseas and English players in our team simply by watching their technique. Conversation: 'South African Lynn?' He referred to scrum half Peter Kirsten of the University of Cape Town. 'The centre who looks at the grass. English?'. He saw the strong running and physical Englishman, Mike Nolan. Pierre had played or coached in most of the rugby playing nations. He was a knowledgeable observer of the specific techniques common in different countries.

It was proving hard for some players, especially the more experienced ones who had learned to play in more structured ways, to accept Pierre's style of play. Those who learned to play in structure found it uncomfortable to make their own decisions as required by the game in movement.

On our return to the UK, the team faced some challenging club teams as well as a visit from the Romanian National team. Pierre visited us for two extended pe-

OURFC 1990

riods of around five days and another stint before the Varsity game. I continued the work on the themes of collective decision making in game play. A month before the Twickenham game, we beat Romania comfortably, playing some ambitious rugby. Oxford used their superior skills and pace in the back line against the more structured Romanians. The toughest test of term was against a Bath team, bristling with international players, including Stuart Barnes, Andy Robinson, John Hall, Jerry

Guscott, and John Webb. We narrowly lost this game, in which we probably had no more than thirty per cent possession. What possession we had we used as fluidly and effectively as possible.

I remember Pierre's final talk with the team before the Varsity Match. The gist was: 'This game presents the biggest challenge mentally. You can play this game as you have already shown, but you have to produce this game under the biggest pressure you have experienced. This is the big stage'. There were two crucial and costly errors, both during the first half, when individuals reverted to 'type', which I would describe as their habitual game. This is always the challenge when trying to change the mental approach for players who have become accustomed to playing in a certain style. Some players under pressure revert to their habitual decision making. We lost the game narrowly, as the two errors seemed to impact adversely on the confidence of the team to play how we had trained. The first error occurred after Oxford had dominated the first fifteen minutes. We had a free kick in the Cambridge twenty-two area. All free kicks were to be taken quickly. The back row would be in deep support of the inside backs, on the call 'un, deux, trois'. The pressure seemed to get to Micky, the scrum half. He tapped and went blind and had his pass intercepted by the Cambridge wing, who was caught only five metres from our line. It was like the wind being blown from our sails. The second error occurred near half time. Our centre had his wing outside him, clear with one defender to beat. He chose the option to beat the defender himself and failed. The relatively short preparation time of around ten weeks was a contributory cause for these errors. Nevertheless, the team scored the most points of any post-war team during the term. The rugby played was both imaginative and exciting. I would find it difficult to change to a more structured approach to coaching. However, I understand the necessity to tailor the needs of the team in a one-off game, to suit the strengths of the selected team.

The captains of OURFC had a powerful role in the organisation and preparation of the club. Player-centred involvement is, I think, important in any rugby club. With the advent of coaching much of that involvement had dissipated. Coaches have become supremoes. From my perspective, it worked well at Oxford, when the captain and I shared a similar vision of our roles and methods of coaching that would benefit the club. During my period in office, there were only two captains with whom I struggled to maintain harmony. I came across several outstanding leaders.

A few captains were unlucky to have a relatively moderate group of players. Even outstanding leadership cannot mask playing deficiencies. Mark Egan, now a Head of Department at World Rugby, was one outstanding captain. His appointment followed an internal wrangle involving the previous year's playing leadership. This situation mirrored the dispute in the Oxford Blues Rowing squad that resulted in a National sporting story and a subsequent book. There was a rebellion within the crew. Mark's mature leadership ensured a quiet resolution of the similar situation in the rugby section. Mark left the door ajar for members of the 'rebel' group. A few felt unable to take the olive branch offered, while others welcomed their return to the team. Mark's team won that year's Varsity game, notable for the high level of teamwork.

Worthy of special mention in that 1990 team was Maru Hiyashi, until then the only Japanese international to represent Oxford. He was the first player I have seen in tears before a game, such was his raised level of emotion. On the field, Maru dislocated his knee. He calmly asked our hooker Errol Norwiech, a medic, if he could put his knee back while on the field.

Other notable captains were Tyrone Howe, a genial Irishman, who went on to play for Ireland and the British Lions; Andrew Everett, a giant, ball playing prop from the University of Cape Town, mature beyond his years, whose idea of a warm up was having sun on his back; Tim O'Brien, who also played for Cambridge; and, as mentioned before, David Henderson and Rupert Vessey. David Henderson embraced the Villepreux way totally and was a ball-playing hooker with an 'edge' to his game. David was a captain who led from the front on the field. Rupert gained the respect of the whole team with his attention to detail and organisational skills. In aspects off the field, he received good support from his secretary Alec Cameron.

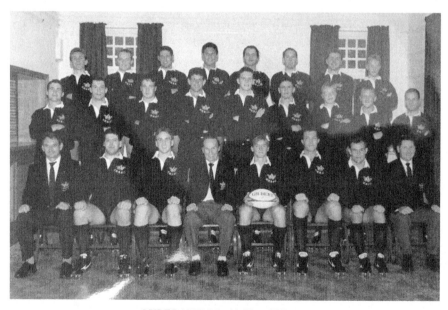

OURFC 1995-96 with Pierre Villepreux

Secretary was a position particular to both universities, a player elected to support the captain in their burdensome administrative duties. Alec doubled up as pack leader, setting an example of commitment on the field to support his impressive administrative skills.

Another special captain was Welshman Simon Griffin, a product of Pontypridd RFC. Simon was very much a player's captain. He performed his social responsibilities as diligently as he displayed his leadership qualities as a marauding flanker. His Varsity victory owed much to whole team commitment. He had a touch of class. One summer evening, as I drove down the High Street in Oxford, I spotted him and a fellow player, Col McDonald. They were in their DJs, sitting around a small table outside University College, sipping champagne and eating burgers from the van parked nearby. They waved me over to join them. A fellow graduate of University College, Neil McDonald, one of the many of the McDonald family to grace the turf at Iffley Road over the years, was a natural leader and forthright captain. He led by example on the field and expected players to show the same commitment.

I was fortunate to meet and become friends with many leading referees during my time coaching OURFC. One of these was the Welsh referee Derek Bevan, who

Playing petanque on the 50th birthday at Ty Gwyn members of the 1988 OURFC tour to Japan elegantly attired in their acquired Japanese 'uniform' includes Duncan Wood, Dai Evans, Andy Williams, David Polkinghorne and Malcolm Brown.

during the late eighties and nineties was among the best referees in world rugby. He stayed at our house after refereeing the annual Stanley's XV against Oxford. The conversation, over a few glasses of wine, went on well into the night, as we reminisced over his many amusing stories. Two of the best English referees of this time were Ed Morrison and Tony Spreadbury. Both of them had that essential gift of top referees, empathy and understanding of the game of rugby. Ed and Tony were regular attendees at coaching conferences we organised in Oxford, as they shared their experiences of the game with coaches. One story that 'Spreaders' told at a conference stood out for me. Two clubs Leicester and Bristol instead of numbering their players' jerseys, used letters. During a particularly physical game, the touch judge called the referee to draw his attention to foul play by a Bristol player. 'Do you have his number?' asked Spreaders, 'Yes,' replied the touch judge, 'number 13.' 'Ah', said Tony, 'we may have an issue here, Bristol are playing with letters on their back!'

There was a considerable Welsh connection to the rugby club. Bryan Morgan, another ex St. Luke's student, was the club administrator for many years, who ensured I did not step out of line. Terry Jones, was the groundsman, whose chickens fertilised the pitch, while his goat, kept the grass in good trim. Low behold any

Mark Egan OURFC capt 1990 and later Head of Development department at World rugby, helping to coach on one of the RFU's roadshows.

players practising on the marked lines of the pitch, if Terry spotted them from the windows of his house, that bordered the ground. Brian Loughman, was a Tutor at University College, and a delightful man, who had such a love and passion for the game. Many recruits to the club came through Brian's connections. Gywndaf Evans, a man of Crymych, was known as the Arthur Dailey of Oxford. Any rugby student requiring a bicycle, refrigerator or any household item, need look no further that the resourceful Gwyndaf. He could also talk for Wales! All of them made considerable contributions to supporting the club.

It was a privilege for me to coach OURFC for fifteen years. I enjoyed working with a range of talents both young and mature. I have remained in touch with many of the players. Many have proceeded to impressive careers in many branches of public and private service. I have tried to indulge in a 'Dream Team' of players representing the Blues in the period 1981 to 1995. I realised it could be two equally competitive teams as shown below.

1. Victor Ubogo (England/Bath) Maru Hyashi (Japan)
2. David Henderson (Scottish Students) Karl Svoboda (Canada)
3. Andrew Everett (University of Cape Town/Western Province) Ian Buckett (Wales) David Penny Canada)
4. Troy Coker (Australia) Neil McDonald (University of Cape Town/Western Province)
5. Bill Campbell (Australia)
6. Brendan Nasser (Australia)
7. Bill Calcraft (Australia) Andy Aitkin (University of Cape Town/Western Province)
8. Mark Egan (Irish Students/Trinity College) Tony Brookes (England Students)
9. David Kirk (New Zealand) Andy Moore (Wales)
10. Stuart Barnes (England and British Lions) David Humphries (Ireland) Brian Smith (Australia)
11. Tyrone Howe (Ireland and British Lions) Steve Barclay (Wales) Derek Wyatt (England)
12. Brendan Mullin (Ireland and British Lions) Simon Halliday (England)
13. David Evans (Wales) Phil Crowe (Australia)
14. Ian Williams (Australia and Japan)) Gary Hein (USA)
15. Rob Egerton (Australia) Hugo MacNeill (Ireland and British Lions)

Most players would be at the university for three to four years. They had the opportunity to play against some of the leading clubs and representative teams, possibly for the only time in their rugby careers. Many players do not continue to play rugby as they launch their careers in well paid jobs but long working hours. As coach I enjoyed helping these players to improve their game. By introducing the players to some new perspectives on how to play the game, I hoped that some would carry these ideas forward when they left the university. Many of these young men would aspire to influential positions in and around their chosen careers. Stuart Barnes has a prominent role in journalism; Simon Halliday and Steve Pearson are leading figures in rugby administration at national level; David Evans works for the Welsh Government to promote in-

David Kirk (left) and Rupert Vessey (right)

ternational sporting events in Wales; others are headteachers in schools; and perhaps the most prestigious of all in rugby administration, Mark Egan, was Head of Game Development for World Rugby. Coaching in this competitive rugby environment helped me to clarify my objectives in a way not possible in club coaching. The challenge of preparing to play a National side does not come for many coaches. Playing an annual one-off game at a high level is a rarity in the game. Making mistakes was part of my learning experience. I met and became friends with many first-class young men. I listened to other coaches, so I was also learning. I worked alongside Chalky White and Pierre Villepreux, the coaches who inspired me with their coaching philosophy. They convinced me that players should participate more fully as part of the coaching process.

The club were often invited to the many out of season seven-à side tournaments in both England and France. A very prestigious tournament was held in Limoges in central France organised by Pierre Villepreux. Teams, mostly from Universities in England, France, Wales, Ireland and Italy competed against French club teams and a side representing the France national team. The year was 1993 and a very pacy Oxford squad under the leadership of Davie Henderson were the stars of the tournament. Along the way we beat Swansea University and had a notable scalp in the French National seven. The impressive trophy, carved from local Limoges stone weighed 'a ton'. It required two players to transport it on our long journey to Oxford.

The most memorable tournament was the inaugural Paris Universities Sevens. It was not the rugby that was so memorable, though Oxford did win the tournament! The celebratory buffet in the evening providing the most extraordinary 'food battle' I have ever witnessed. Our very gifted international group contained two South Africans, two Australians, two Englishmen including our captain, Rupert Vessey an Irishman and a Welshman.

The French buffet was sumptuous. There was a copious amount of food. The amount of food and wine available could have fed a small army. The evening soiree, held in a large hall in the University, started in a very civilised way, with teams mixing and conversing about the rugby event. We have to remember this was a group of rugby playing students, just having finished two days of playing in a physically demanding sevens tournament. As the wine flowed, inhibitions began to disappear.

The French hosts began to lob a few bread rolls towards random groups of players. The escalation of food began to intensify. Our experienced post graduates, led by Rob Egerton, sensed events were only going to deteriorate quickly. A rapid council of war was held, and in true Oxford heroic tradition, it was decided to stage a tactical retreat. We moved quietly away from the centre of the action, to the periphery and hid behind an overturned table.

The food, including some liquids by now was flying around the room with greater intensity. National pride was being stirred. The Italians using throw and run techniques, the Spanish, the most glamorous of fighters seemed to enjoy the whole event, and the Irish, with national pride at stake led most of the counter attacks. It was all out war!

The Oxford group were now deciding how to address a deteriorating situation, when large quantities of water spray began to appear. A fire hose had been detached from the wall and I believe it was the French who were manipulating the hose with great effect. The Oxford retreat was carried out in great haste as we fled through a back door. The mixture of food and alcohol with rugby playing students rarely ends in peace and goodwill!

We made our way to the West Bank in Paris. Our guitar playing Irishman entertained us and the customers of the Parisian bar with some soothing Irish ballads, that helped to calm the memories of the earlier events.

I continued coaching OURFC until 1995, when the University committee decided to appoint a full-time coach. My contract had been on a twenty-hours a week basis. The other half of my role, after 1990, was with the RFU, as one of their Youth Development Officers. During that time, I served two employers. The OURFC advertised nationally for the position of Director of Rugby. I applied, but contemplated whether my age, I was fifty-eight, or my accomplishments would be a factor in the selection process. In the event, the appointment, from a prestigious group of applicants, went to Steve Hill, current coach of Richmond. I, therefore, applied to the RFU for a full-time position as Youth Development Officer, which Oxfordshire RFU had wanted. I was now to immerse myself in developing the youth programme in the county. Though wanting to take a break from team coaching, after much persuading, I took on the position as head coach to Chinnor Rugby Club. This ambitious club is on the outskirts of Thame, ten miles from Oxford. So began another phase in my rugby career.

LONDON WELSH *v* OXFORD

LONDON WELSH		OXFORD
(Colours—Red)		*(Colours— Green, Black and Silver)*
J. P. R. Williams †	Full Back	A. Barraclough 15
T. G. R. Davies †	Threequarters	N. C. W. Furley 14
K. Hughes †		P. R. E. McFarland 13
S. J. Dawes †		L. R. Evans 12
J. L. Shanklin †		D. S. Gilgour 11
D. Llewellyn	Fly Half	R. P. Tapper 10
W. G. Hullin †	Scrum Half	Bagnall (Capt.) 9
A. R. Pender		J. F. Mawle 1
A. P. Baker		M. Whiteside 2

27 Great P

Enjoy L

Separate Lounge Bar a

PRIVATE FUNCTIONS DINNERS SUPPERS BUFFETS MEETINGS

the players w…

Alan Barraclough, full-back, … Formerl…
at Durham University.

Nigel Furley, wing, 5′ 9″, 11st. Oxfordshire County player. …n University…

Paddy McFarland, centre, 5′ 11″, 12st. Oxford Blue 1967, Oxfordshire County playe…
Formerly with Rosslyn Park and London Irish.

Lynn Evans, centre, 5′ 9½″, 11st. An Oxfordshire County player who has played for Cros…
Keys. Captain and leading points scorer last season. Has appeared 165 times in the 1st XV…

Duncan Kilgour, wing, 5′ 11″, 11st 3lb. …hire County captain. Leading try score…
last season. N… …nty football with Oxford, Hertford an…
…s. Is an England Schoolboy Internation…
148 games with the 1st XV.

8lb. 220 1st XV. appearances. Oxfor…

…n of the Club with 155 1st XV. appea…
…ties.

…yed for Eastern Counties and Norfoll…
…nty player and former England S-…

…shire Coun…

The Oxford…
Thursday 7's s…

Because of the …
numbers to issue…
hands of the prin…
out as planned, w… … Newpo…
game, and the app… …s that all our seve…
Lions have now se… …k of them appear today. W…
extend a hearty we… …to Lions captain John Dawes, who h…
this year relinquish… …on Welsh after six historic years at the heln…
All lovers of this gr… …guy will have heard with regret of John's decision to qu…
the international sce… …everybody on the ground today will, we feel sure, wish to take th…
opportunity to join us in saying "Thanks for everything, John !"

* * *

The records this season of the two sides when we went to press were :—

	P	W	D	L	For	Agst.

OXFORDSHIRE

15 P. R. CARROLL   Harlequins

14 M. F. DOUCH   Bedford

13 I. RAY   Sussex University

12 L. R. EVANS   Oxford

11 D. S. KILGOUR   Oxford (C

10 D. R. S

 9 D. B

 1 M. FO

 2 M. WHI

 3 J. F. MA

 4 J. S. HAR

 5 A. P. HALL

        SA

J.R.

THE PROTEAS

24 S. I. BRUIN

22 W. E. WI

3 H. L.

1 J. A.

RUGBY STAGE DE LA LIGUE CORSE

Un professeur no

Légende du rugby, le Gallois, ancien joueur
et entraîneur d'Oxford notamment, occupe
un poste de cadre à la RFU. Il est en Corse
à l'invitation de la ligue régionale

Du jeu simple, à

A 79 ans, Lynn Evans est une légende bien vivante du rugby.
Le Gallois fut d'abord joueur
à Oxford, avant d'en devenir un des
plus fameux coaches pendant quin-
ze saisons. Il prit aussi place sur le
banc de Littlemore, de Chinor et dé-

d'entraînement. Les Anglais sont si
forts aujourd'hui grâce à des hom-
mes comme Lynn Evans. Forts dans
la méthodologie analytique, dans
la technique individuelle et dans la
communication sur le terrain. C'est
important ça le décisionnaire dans

ceux inscrits d
Teullière.
"C'est vrai qu
est capitale, c
Gracieuse Ma
autant maîtris
verbale que n

nmé Lynn Evans

, aux pieds et aussi de la communication sont les marques de fabrique de ce membre de la RFU.

/ PHOTOS C.L.

championnat

mmunication
e sujet de Sa
Mais il faut
mmunication
ale, savoir in-

(Lacombe). Dans le monde moderne le coaching doit changer, c'est un sport qui évolue sans cesse. C'est ce qui me plaît encore aujourd'hui. Mes méthodes ne séduisent pas toujours mais lorsqu'un coach les adopte, je vous assure, qu'il ne veut plus

ballon à la main toucher les joueurs de l'équipe d'en face. Les gamins ont le sourire. Sam Lacombe, caméra en main, aussi : "ce ne sont pas des exercices que l'on fait. Là, ça permet, en restant très ludique de bien dissocier le haut et le bas du corps.

RFU AND
PENGUINS INTERNATIONAL COACHING

'As a young coach it was hard. I did not believe in the 'motivating coach', but
the hard-working coach who leads by example. The players were asked to take
more responsibility. They were not used to it. Most if not all the players were
coming from coaching environments where they were not asked to take much
responsibility'

Wayne Smith – New Zealand Coach

After working for nearly thirty years in the teaching profession, I combined a
part-time teaching role with a managerial role at the Peers school-based leisure centre. I needed a different challenge. My opportunity arose when the RFU commenced
a youth development scheme in 1990. The RFU combined with other interested
parties, such as local councils, the National Sports Council and local businesses, to
fund this new scheme. All the counties and boroughs in England appointed youth
development officers (YDOs). The scheme entailed a rolling ten-year programme.
Oxfordshire linked with Oxford University (a constituent body of the RFU) to provide me with a coaching role at the university and a YDO role for the county. The
job description suited my qualifications. I was already coaching OURFC and was a
senior coach for the RFU. I would be paid for working in rugby. The university also
provided free office facilities. I left teaching in July 1990 and commenced my new
position, later that year, at the start of the new rugby season.

As I now had two separate roles, I needed to allocate my time to suit the needs of
both employers. Accordingly, during the autumn term, I gave more time to OURFC,
ahead of the Varsity match taking place in early December. Most of the youth development work occurred during the school day, on a practical level. I worked with
the local rugby clubs on a Sunday. In 1991, England hosted the second Rugby World
Cup. The high-profile players at OURFC were really helpful in supporting local
school events. The main World Cup event for the County was a Tag Rugby tournament, involving over twenty primary schools. The local football league team, Oxford United (with future England football manager Steve McClaren) and OURFC
(Including David Kirk, New Zealand captain in the first world cup) took part in a
penalty shoot-out both in football and in rugby. The rugby team did not even get
close! This was no great surprise as professional footballers spend most of their
time kicking a ball in a multitude of ways. University players often accompanied
me on our frequent visits to schools to promote rugby. We assisted clubs to link with
their local school. Audley Lumsden (future England full-back) was particularly no-

table for eating most of the promotional fried noodles intended for the children. Audley loved game-style coaching as he could display his intuitive skills and joy of running with the ball.

During my role as YDO, I took an increasing part in the coaching programme to develop the RFU's young YDOs. This included courses in the various regions of

Coaching at a primary school in the Oxford area

England. I would outline practices and principles for the coaches to do more game-based coaching. In conjunction with the Southern Region Sports Council, and the very supportive chief officer David Dolman, I proposed forming a South Region Elite Development Squad for leading U15 players. This was a first attempt by the region to expose young players to the game-based approach. One of the aims was to see if players learned better with less structured coaching processes. We selected the thirty players taking part, by using skill-based tests. These players then attended a week long residential course at the National Sports Centre at Bisham Abbey. Following the course, they attended monthly revision sessions of two hours. During the residential course we observed how the boys responded to unfamiliar. coaching methods. Both the players and the coaches found the first two days were quite tough. It is always a major issue for players moving from a structured method of coaching into a more decision-based coaching style. Players feel comfortable in drill-based coaching led by the coach, but when put into a games-based practice frequently struggle to find the best options. My fellow YDOs from the Counties were familiar with the coaching methods. The game understanding of the boys began to emerge on day three. This was when they began to link more passages of play together with fewer breakdowns. It was quite remarkable, by the last day of the course, to see more players taking effective decisions in the game. They were recognising where,

My mentor and friend the great Chalkie White ponders while working with the rugby development officers of the South-west region

when, how and why it was easier to penetrate some gaps than others. The feedback from the boys was mostly along the lines 'We have not been coached like this before and we found it challenging, but now we are beginning to understand it'. The weakness of the course happened to be the infrequent follow up sessions. The players would go back to clubs where structured coaching was the norm. They would soon revert to a more structured approach to play. We needed more creative coaches!

I would place H.V. 'Chalky' White on a par with Pierre Villepreux, as one of the most influential coaches in my career. Chalky began working for the RFU as regional administrator for the South-West Region after leaving his role as an inspirational and successful coach of Leicester RFC. If Chalky believed you were enthusiastic to improve as a coach, he would find the time to guide, nurture, question, and support you. Many an evening, late into the night, I stayed up listening to anecdotes and reminiscences of his life as a coach.

Three particular coaching sessions Chalky conducted, as regional manager to his YDOs, stand out. Firstly, he had brought a New Zealand open-side flanker Willie Phillips, to our meeting in a hotel in Newbury. His detailed questioning of the player about what, how and why he made decisions on the field, opened our eyes to the detail such a player possessed. His questioning of Willie explored his thinking on what clues in the game enabled the player to choose the best options more often. He replied, 'My coaching and hard practice in New Zealand had been so detailed, that over time I began to make the better choices.' There are few shortcuts in this game. His early experiences, in a rugby mad country, had equipped him with a detailed foundation on which to build his adult playing career.

Secondly, a lineout catching practice, held at Taunton School, required the observer to look at the detail of the whole jump, from preparation to jump until delivery of the ball. It was fascinating to realise how general most of the YDOs observations were. They lacked the clarity needed to analyse efficient movement and skill. Some of the questions Chalky posed included: 'How and where is the thrust applied to ensure the maximum lift?' 'Is the ball caught with both hands at the same time or do you notice if one hand is a controller of the ball?'. 'In what way does the jumper control the delivery of the ball to the scrum half?' I learned more about these skills in an hour with Chalky than I had in the whole of my previous playing and coaching career.

Thirdly, this time on the beach at Bude in North Cornwall, we had the privilege of listening to Graham Dawe, (Bath and England hooker and fierce competitor), give a detailed description of the hooker's role in the scrum. As usual, Chalky's incisive questions enhanced our understanding. 'How do you change the binding to get closer to the ball?' 'What practices do you have to improve your speed of strike?' 'In what ways do your props contribute to putting pressure on the opposition?' We gained so much more detail on the technical parts of the game, which helped to make us better coaches. That questioning was probably harder for Graham than packing down against an international front row. When Chalky finally retired from the RFU, I decided our region needed to continue with this technical work. Together with Simon Hardy, the new regional manager, we continued the coaching sessions for YDOs. My special area was coaching the 'game in movement.' Within a few years, Simon became a specialist lineout coach for England. The age of specialised coaching was upon us.

Every January, our region hosted a coaching evening headed up by Des Diamond, one of the London Regional managers. It was often my task to look for coaches from other sports to present on game principles that could relate to rugby. One such presenter was Wai Taumaunu, the National Coach of the New Zealand netball team. Her brief was developing peripheral vision. Being a New Zealander, Wai was more than familiar with rugby. She gave a very insightful presentation of how players could become more aware of game situations through using a series of practices familiar to the netball game. This capacity, to scan and read situations in games, is generally a major weakness in rugby. Too often players do not scan ahead before receiving the ball. They continue to look straight ahead, rather than move their eyes to assess other options. Coaches should see how other invasion games have similar, attacking concepts of 'go forward and support'. Developing players' perception within game situations is not a strength in our coaching of rugby.

On one occasion, the GB national basketball coach, a Hungarian named Lazlo Nemeth, who had never seen a game of rugby, gave a presentation on developing ball and movement skills. He illustrated the skills and some small sided game practices used with his players, who ranged from beginners to elite Olympic athletes. The work was intensive and progressively more demanding. We observed U16 age group players trying to master skipping rope moves of increasing complexity. Very few could do even the most basic forms of skipping. We should be looking to see what high level coaches are doing in other sports and be more prepared to see how these skills could enhance our game. Lazlo went to see two training sessions of rugby in Leeds, before the course. One was in rugby union and the other in rugby league. His comment about the comparisons between rugby and basketball was very perceptive and one that a rugby coach was unlikely to make. He said, 'The big problem for both games are the same, the turnover, where both teams have to immediately re-adjust from defence to attack and vice-versa'.

A third presenter was another New Zealander, Wayne Smith. At the time, Wayne was head coach at Northampton RFC. His presentation, on looking at ball retention and the principles involved, was notable for its clarity and simplicity. His practical session was a master class in relating the practices to the game. During all of his practices, Wayne spent time assessing the whole situation, before posing a challenging question for the player. He welcomed my request to bring the younger YDOs in the region to watch a Northampton training session. Such openness is not often seen in rugby clubs. Wayne spent much time with the YDOs, answering their questions. It was the first time I had seen players who played in the same position coaching each other. This session occurred at the end of the training, Pierre had influenced Wayne, during their time in Italy, when Wayne coached in Treviso. They have remained close friends ever since that time and meet up whenever Wayne comes to Europe.

As my contacts with high level coaches expanded, I invited some to run coach education sessions at the university. Bob Dwyer, who was coaching at Leicester at the time, gave a stimulating session on the importance of honing ball skills to the highest level possible. The success of the Australian team during Bob's reign as coach, was evidence of a high-speed game. His team played with the maximum of accuracy in skills and decision making. Their World Cup win in 1991 was no accident. John Eales, the former Australian captain, did a lineout clinic at Iffley Road. John was elegantly attired in blue jeans, suede shoes and a sweater for the practi-

John Moore Welsh rugby scrum coach conducting a coaching session at Iffley Road Oxford

cal work. It did not distract from his practical session. This practice was notable because John's natural skills were so innate, that he often struggled to explain his technique. Asked how he controlled his jump and catch, he replied, 'I don't know mate, I just jump and catch it and deliver it'. John's nickname was, 'Nobody', in that 'Nobody is perfect!' Simple!

In the early '90s, the RFU invited me to become a staff coach. At that time, this was the highest coaching level available. One of my tasks was to staff some of the residential coaching courses at Bisham. These were week-long courses for the equivalent of today's Level 3 award. Within Oxfordshire, I led courses for those beginning their coaching journey. I participated in a new initiative run by the RFU on mentoring coaches aspiring to reach Level 3. The RFU provided training to ensure that we gave the best possible experience for the ambitious coaches. At the same time, the governing body wanted to improve the quality of the coaching courses. The change entailed a move away from the usual, coach-led methods. The move was to a more player-centred style, giving players more involvement in the learning process. For example, instead of telling a player to relax his shoulders when passing, to avoid tension in that area of the body, the coach would ask a question such as. 'Tell me where you think your hands finish as you complete the pass?' Now the player would feed-back information to the coach and take some control of his learning. This positive work still continues. Players appear more satisfied and learn more efficiently when they own more of the learning process. Gerald Davies, former British Lions player, said that Carwyn James' methods made the player feel that he was owning the learning process.

Also, in the '90s, the RFU asked me to lead courses overseas, when they received requests from abroad. I spent a three month 'sabbatical' in the USA and Canada. The aim was to support the development of coaches and players in the high school and college game. The period spent in the States was particularly exciting. I travelled north to south and east to west, under the careful management of Katie Wurst, an impressive American women's coach, Katie was remarkable. She ensured that I left and arrived on time, in my many destinations, as I criss-crossed the USA every four or five days. Katie was open to learning. She found the questioning style of coaching very stimulating. I experienced coaching one of the teams in Washington DC. They played their rugby on parkland, near the White House. There were no changing rooms and no toilets. They just had a pitch but one with an iconic background. There was a first experience of coaching mixed groups of fifteen-year olds contact rugby in Maryland. Asking their coach if it was okay for contact work, he said he was sometimes worried about the boys getting hurt.

Watching the annual National Colleges' tournament, played in Albuquerque, gave me an overall picture of the standard of College rugby. I saw, also, the inequality of the game. UCLA arrived in their luxury coach complete with state-of-the-art kit. Their opponents, Chicago University, had travelled all day and night, from the North to the South of the USA, in a minibus. The coaching courses I ran in California, Maryland, Houston and Nashville, Tennessee were other highlights of a remarkable tour.

I held coaching sessions in high schools. Many of these were Jesuit schools situated in the Washington area. The Jesuit community appeared to view rugby as a contributor to improving life skills. Previously, the boys had received the structured method of coaching. After a couple of hours coaching through the player-centred approach, the decision making of the boys had improved considerably. Phases of continuity increased to a stage where stoppages had decreased by up to half.

Perhaps, the highlight of the tour was my attending and presenting at the USA Rugby Annual Coaching Conference. This conference was held in San Jose, California. Lynn Kidman, who has been a leading figure in the Worldwide Teaching Games for Understanding (TGFU) movement, and who has written books on the topic, is an advocate of games-related coaching. During one of the indoor sessions,

My big moment on stage at a club in Nashville Tennessee. What great guys.

Mary, my wife responded to a request to complete one small group session on mul-ti-input issues. She was the star of the group, displaying a capacity to listen and ab-sorb more than one thing at a time. The purpose of the exercises was to help the lis-tener to pick out the key and relevant points that the players constantly have to deal with in complex decision-making situations. They need to find the most relevant and effective solutions, under considerable time pressures. The practical, outdoor work was on a showground being prepared for the massive State Fair, taking place the next day. The place was a hive of activity. The American coaches appreciated the player-centred practical work. Lynn Kidman, no rugby player herself, engaged fully in the practical work.

I went on to Canada. Here, I gave a presentation at the TGFU Conference, held at the University of British Columbia in Vancouver. This was a unique opportunity to share a coaching philosophy with academics and presenters across a range of sports. I trust my contribution did something to further the cause of my approach for rugby. My presentation centred around showing video clips of beginners learn-ing to play rugby. Then, I posed questions to the audience about what they observed. 'How was the learning taking place?' After observing the clips, I asked the attend-ees an open question about what they saw. This led to further discussion on the role of the coach and how the players were learning, if the input from the coach was minimal. I used the same method with my audience as I would have used if I had been coaching the players.

The vast distance between British Columbia and Ontario highlights the challenges Canada faces in the development of the game nationally. I did some interesting work with Gareth Rees, former Oxford University and Canadian international, with whom I stayed, while in Vancouver. This work centred around game-based coaching. The U18 players were more adaptive and learned more quickly than adult players. It is vital to start players at a young age with game-based coaching. I returned, on two occasions, to Canada, both times with Pierre. On the first trip to Vancouver, in January, the rain poured throughout the two-day course. This forced us to present the 'game of movement 'in a sports hall. That was a challenge. Close support of the ball carriers on their feet was essential in order to retain possession and to go forward. I always found that playing on hard surfaces was a remarkable incentive to stay on one's feet. The sudden curtailment of this trip was the result of me eating some infected oysters. This left me in bed for two days. Pierre, serenely unaffected by the oysters, finished the course.

The second trip, to Ontario, took place in the depths of a Canadian winter. It entailed a coaching course at the Canadian Military College indoor centre in Kingston, which was double the size of our previous venue. Pierre, myself and Gary Henderson, Head of RFU Coaching presented different aspects of the movement game. Gary and I worked on some technical work relevant to the tactical objectives of the game. One example was to practise making offloading passes, with the objective of providing opportunities to use offloads in the game. Canadian coaches, particularly the teachers, were eager to discuss the merits of the game style of coaching.

In the mid-eighties I received an invitation to coach in Heidelberg. I took with me Hugo MacNeill, Irish and British Lion and OURFC captain at the time. Heidelberg had a rugby-playing history of over a hundred years, but the game remained a minor sport in Germany. There were about six teams within the city, excluding university sides. Our objective was to raise the understanding of the 'game in movement'. We tried to achieve this through coaches playing in the game. They were able to experience the challenges faced by players through immersion in the learning process. This method was effective in getting the coaches to understand what the challenges were for the players. They made the same mistakes! It was a difficult task for adults, more familiar with a structured game. Sometimes you can only plant the seeds. Our very friendly German hosts certainly taught us a thing or two about fine wines and beers.

By the early part of the new millennium I had forged a close friendship with Didier Retiere. He was a development officer, working for the French Rugby Federation (FFR,) and was, at that time, coach of the French U20 team. Didier later became forwards coach of the French team that lost narrowly to the All Blacks in the final of the 2011 World Cup in New Zealand. Didier's coaching of set pieces applied similar principles to the 'game in movement.' He used a tactical approach. In lineouts, he would start with competitive activities in small-sided games. For example, on a one v one throw in, a player would try to lose his marker through movement or feinting. The sessions were lively and active. Decision making was the central theme. Players tried to anticipate outcomes without signals from the thrower. The complexity increased but the game-based challenge remained. The same procedure occurred with scrums. The one v one competition remained with some input of a technical nature but still game based. Players then progressed to two v two and three v three. The tactical input was always evident. The objectives included how to destabilise your opponent and how to improve your balance.

I invited Didier to England on a number of occasions. One was a memorable visit to Cornwall for their annual coaches' day. The Cornish coaches relished his game-based, lineout coaching. On another visit, he made a presentation to senior coaches at the RFU national coaching conference. Coaches valued these presentations because they demonstrated how to coach the set pieces through game activities. Didier prioritised the tactical over the technical input. I had the pleasure of meeting up with Don Rutherford again, following his retirement to enjoy the delights of Cornwall with his family.

I visited a French U18 coaching camp held in St. Lary, high up in the Pyrenees. The coaching philosophy of using game activity, taught as closely as possible to an actual game, became very clear to me. It was evident that the game play was done in a dynamic high intensity way. What was not so clear to me, when a young English coach, accompanying me, suggested that we challenge Didier and his assistant coach, to a canoe race down the fast-flowing mountain river situated near the camp. We lasted about ten yards, before capsizing and breaking the world under water downhill canoeing record. We bounced off numerous rocky projections. I learned that it was not always wise to listen to young inexperienced coaches, especially those with minimal knowledge of rapid water canoeing.

A visit to Moscow to coach at the Moscow Academy Institute, the home of space exploration in Russia, was quite memorable. A conducted tour of the early spacecrafts, preserved within the Institute but not on public display, was particularly impressive. The Institute had invited me to visit after I coached a session for their rugby team, during their visit to Oxford on a UK tour. I stayed in the students' accommodation at the university. Even though it was April, the snowy weather determined that we had to conduct coaching sessions indoors. Trying to maintain the concepts of 'rugby in movement' while coaching indoors was very demanding. I tried to find activities that made the players use every centimetre of the space in which they had to play. Literally, every half metre made all the difference between the attack going forward or stopping. Running lines had to be straight and precise, Evasion skills were essential to open up even a small gap in the defence. In limited space, accuracy was vital as time pressure was intense. Immediate and close support was essential in order to keep continuity in the game. Quick release of the ball in contact offered greater chances to go forward, as the defence had less time to reorganise. Immediate support of the ball was easier but so it was for the defence to stop as space was limited. Looking after the ball carrier was a priority. For experienced coaches, a coaching session taken in a limited space provided considerable challenges. The coach must utilise every square centimetre of space. You realise how valuable small spaces become. It will be necessary to limit the numbers on the playing area but rapid and regular substituting of players helps keep everyone involved. Coaches should provide chances for the players to become more aware of how to make space and how to preserve space in limited areas. In the modern game, we hear complaints from professional teams about the suffocation of space by too many defenders. Coaches should minimise the space used in team training. Thereby, the players would make better use of the extra space available on match day. I think we made useful progress, when we went outside, to play on an artificial surface. The players opened up more gaps using their improved running lines. Conversely, a few players used the extra space to run sideways. Well, Rome was not built in one day. An enemy was the neat vodka that one was obliged to consume.

Another close friend at the RFU was a fellow St. Luke's College man, Tony Robinson. He casually e-mailed me to ask if I wanted to do some coaching in Malaysia with the Penguins. The Penguins, formed in 1959, were an invitational side that travelled the world playing and coaching and had travelled to many different countries. Under the sponsorship of HSBC, they offered Coach and Referee formal education courses based on the International Rugby Board courses. So, I went to Kuala Lumpur, along with Gary Henderson, the head of the RFU's community coaching programme. During the next ten years, I visited Malaysia regularly, to run coaching courses for teachers. Our base in Kuala Lumpur was the Hilton Hotel. Comfort was not a problem. We held two coaching courses outside the capital. Both were at stunning venues, not normally used for coaching rugby. The first venue was near a beach in Eastern Malaysia in a place called Cherating. Conducting part of the course on the beach and the rest on a school field, was a definite first for me. Chasing a monkey off the roof of my beach hut was a new experience. The other trip was to Borneo. Here our venue was close to the jungle. The tropical rain came every day. One memory stands out from that course. During a warm up the players were conducting among themselves, they all broke into a rhythmic dance, moving to their mesmeric humming sounds. Maybe we could learn something from that. I must mention the very genial host and main organiser on the ground, a lovely man called Charlie Wong, a member of Cobra Rugby Club in KL, who lived and breathed rugby. He always looked out for me. Malaysia is one of many Asian countries trying to further their development in the game. However, as is often the case, governance and shortage of finance are considerable obstacles for their progress. Game-based coaching would accelerate the understanding of the game in countries like Malaysia.

The Far East provided me with experience of rugby in two countries. One had links to the UK and the other was under the control of the USA. The former British Colony of Hong Kong, now under Chinese rule, has a long tradition of playing rugby. Guam, a USA dependency, has only recent experience of the game. While attending the Hong Kong Sevens, I found out that the family of a former Governor of Hong Kong, who played a prominent role in making the Hong Kong Sevens the global attraction it is today, was closely related to my son-in-law, Calum. As a result of my connections, a seat in the President's box and a visit to the former Governor's house were special experiences.

Along with Steve Hill, then coach at OURFC, we spent a day in Guangzhou, coaching the People's Republican Army squad. Having a whole day to coach, we spent time moving from game play to technical practice and helping the players to link the two. We made progress with their decision options, but really needed an extended time to lay firmer foundations. If China harnessed their considerable human resources, they would become a force in World Rugby. It will happen one day. The officers of the Army were more than generous hosts. I had to ask Steve if he would drink my toast of the local spirit. I was unable to keep up with a toast every ten minutes during our meal.

We flew out a few days later. My wife, Mary, was again accompanying me. We landed at 5 a.m. on Guam. On transfer to the hotel, we found that, from the high-rise hotel, we were overlooking a most stunning beach and clear ocean. There was an American rugby development officer on the island. There were few opportunities for him and fellow coaches to share ideas and rugby knowledge with the world beyond Guam. I held many conversations with them and the leading administrators. We held coaching clinics to pursue ways to aid the progress of rugby. Together, we prepared a long-term development plan that suited the needs of the Guam Rugby Union. A particularly encouraging aspect of the rugby was the increasing number of women playing the game. Mary and I awoke one night, during the stay, to a rumbling and shaking in the hotel. A minor earthquake was taking place. I learned that these occurrences are quite frequent and are very scary ten floors above ground.

Coaching in countries closer to home was always interesting. In the UK and Ireland, I made several visits to support coach education projects. In Ireland, a Penguin coaching visit entailed coaching players who were taking part in a club age group festival in Dublin. Brian O'Driscoll was the guest presenter. The Penguin coaches conducted specific sessions with individual teams. These were mostly skill-based warm up sessions. The Penguin coaches were supporting individual teams with skill work. This, probably, was not the ideal use of our coaching expertise. The main priority for the teams was, naturally, the tournament. This was not an event for coaching new techniques.

I made two differing visits at the invitation of the Scottish RFU. One was to promote an excellent publication, produced by the Union, on game-related warm up skills. I presented several examples of such practices, at the event held at Ayr rugby club. I did a completely different presentation in Edinburgh with the academy group of the Edinburgh professional team. It was very revealing for me to see the U20 squad play in the game style I advocate. I asked the coaches present to observe some key areas of the game. 'What do the players normally do when I give them the ball to commence the actions?' 'What is the usual action in contact?' ''What is the normal shape of the attack?' The answer, briefly, to the first question was 'Run immediately to the defence'. The second answer was 'Go immediately to the ground'. The third answer was 'Shape is normally a flat line'. Support of the ball normally was rarely from the deep axis. It showed the patterns of attack were relatively programmed. We had an interesting debate after the session, when we talked about possible changes. The players were skilful. When we tried different practices, they made good progress in keeping the ball alive. They used more evasive footwork and deep support on the ball carrier. The Scottish RU have been leading advocates in trying to increase ball in play time. They have done this by encouraging their age group players to play in games with limited stoppages at set pieces. This approach is successful, as Scottish rugby is flourishing at age group level with a more innovative style of rugby.

On a particular visit to Cardiff on the invitation of John Schropfer, Head of Welsh Rugby Coach Development, I conducted a session on the principles of the 'game in movement'. The coaches generally found it challenging to apply the appropriate principles, when actually playing in the game. That was not surprising for players unfamiliar with that style. When they led practices to address some of the problems experienced in the game, it was mostly through drills rather than more game-like practices. Further Penguin visits took place in Gibraltar, to aid coach de-

*Sitting under the portrait of Nelson Mandela's in the bungalow in which he stayed
before release from Paarle Prison*

velopment; in Parma in Italy, to run a Level two IRB coaching award; and to Dubai, to introduce rugby to primary schools.

The longest and most productive visit I had was to South Africa, during the British Lions tour in 2009. A team of 8 coaches from England, Scotland, Wales, Fiji and New Zealand covered 1 month in two shifts in South Africa in support of the HSBC sponsored Lions tour. The main focus of the trip was conducting IRB coaching courses in the major cities of Johannesburg, Bloemfontein, Port Elizabeth, Durban and Cape Town. The coaches in the first two venues were not comfortable with mixed race groupings. This was not an issue in the southern cities of the country. While in Bloemfontein, we observed a game of 15-a-side at U9. All players were bare footed. The game included scrums, lifting in the lineout and all laws of the adult game. As soon as the game began, all thirty players converged around the ball. As the game progressed, the biggest and fastest players dominated. A number of players did not even touch the ball. The physio was the busiest person on the field, as hit after hit went on. I now see that selection for the national side begins early, with the elimination of the weak and the promotion of the fast and strong players to the next level.

The stand out moment of the tour was the coaching course we conducted at Paarl prison near Cape Town. This course was for the inmates of the prison. They were participating in a ground-breaking scheme looking at rehabilitating the young men to make it easier to start a new life outside. They took part in other sports as well. The early signs were encouraging. These young men, many of whom were illiterate and products of the violent townships, were making remarkable progress. The warden in charge of the scheme said their behaviour, motivation, and education were all improving. He felt that their chances of a decent life outside were more achievable. What was special about our rugby course, was the active participation of the British rugby press on the course who were in South Africa covering the British Lions rugby tour. Their support of the young men was impressive as they joined in the practical sessions. During the theory lessons. Eddie Butler and Owen Slot were among the coaches. Paarl Prison was where Nelson Mandela finally gained release from his prison sentence. One of the warders, who cared for Mandela in those last months, took us on a conducted tour of the house in which he stayed and met representatives of the ruling South African government. To learn the story of those last months was quite remarkable and very moving.

Inmates at Paarl Prison

Two other interesting visits were to Malta and Luxembourg. The latter country's population doubles each day as workers enter the country and halves by late evening. In Luxembourg, I presented a video for coaches looking at examples from games in which coaching in game-based movement was evident. These examples showed players taking relevant choices of action according to the positions of the defenders and supporters of the ball carrier. Pierre, in his role as Western European coach educator, organised this course. In Malta, I worked with the small number of coaches on the island. I had the opportunity to do more individual work with the coaches. I find this one-to-one work stimulates both coaches. Helping a coach on an individual level for an extended time is not normally available on courses with large numbers of coaches. The Maltese international shirt I received has joined those tucked away in my special shirts drawer at home.

This period of my coaching career enabled me to travel to many countries and to support the development of the game worldwide. It gave me greater insight into the difficulties faced by emerging rugby nations, who are managing on limited financial and human resources. World Rugby faces immense challenges trying to bridge the huge gap between the relatively wealthy nations with established rugby traditions and the unpaid officials of countries wishing to grow the game. From a coaching perspective, I believe firmly that a game-based coaching approach develops a game understanding much more quickly than structured procedures. Some recent work, by Pierre Villepreux in Madagascar, with complete beginners to rugby, demonstrates that within a few hours of game-based coaching, the young (13 to15 years old) were playing a very recognisable game of rugby. I am sure that this method is the most effective way to develop players' tactical awareness.

When you meet someone in a far-flung corner of the world, while travelling on a rugby related event, you realise you have been living a rather long time.

During an extended stay in Australia for the 2003 Rugby World Cup my wife and I experienced several 'chance' meetings. Max Boyce was due to perform at the Sydney Opera House, so we eagerly queued up to buy tickets for his concert. Sadly, sold out! So, Madame Butterfly it had to be. As we continued to queue a voice behind me called, 'Is that Lynn Evans?'. I turned to see a man with little hair left on this head who I did not immediately recognise. He could see I did not immediately recognise him. 'It's Paddy McFarlane, we played together for Oxford and the County'. Embarrassed, I apologised for not recognising him, but he just smiled and pointed to his head. The next twenty minutes were spent reflecting on past rugby experiences.

The following week while still in Sydney but now with Rob Egerton, the former Aussie full back we were in the fish market. A voice from some distance away, with a distinct French accent, called out 'Lin what are you doing here?'. It was Fabrice Bouchard a coaching friend of Pierre Villepreux. I refrained from saying 'I was looking for fish', as he continued to say 'Pierre is here too'. A long coffee break took place soon after.

On an earlier trip to Australia, my wife and daughters were watching a hockey game in Perth sat in the stand. when a young lady sitting close by, asked if I was

Lynn Evans who did coaching courses at Westminster College in Oxford. I replied in the affirmative and she reflected on how much she enjoyed being involved in the course. The chances of meeting by sheer chance on the other side of the world must be fairly remote.

During the 2003 World Cup Mary and me had taken a break organised by my Aussie rugby friend Brendan Nasser, for a few days on the Gold Coast. One evening Mary and myself were enjoying a meal in one of the outside restaurants near the sea, when I glanced over to see a gentleman around my age, who I thought I recognised. After consulting with Mary we concluded it was Budge Rogers, the former England flanker. I had played against him once for Oxford against Bedford. I ventured over and introduced myself and the three of us spent the rest of the evening drinking some excellent Australian red.

Changing continents, we now move to South Africa where I was coaching for the Penguins and seeing some Lions rugby. Mary and I were in a hotel in Port Elisabeth, and were waiting in the breakfast queue, when Mary heard what she thought was a familiar voice. We turned around and saw this rather well-built man, who we immediately recognised as Roger Powell, a second row forward who played with in Oxford, and later joined Llanelli, following a job move to Wales. He partnered the great Derek Quinell in the second row and even managed an England trial. He was startled when we waved at him. The rest of the morning was spent touring the area together and reminiscing on rugby and our social life.

Following the Lions test match against South Africa at Durban in 2008, Mary and me were taking a flight to Port Elisabeth to continue the coaching tour of the country. Sitting quietly in the café and glanced over to see an older version of a young fly half I had coached at Oxford. Stuart Barnes, covering the tour as the Times rugby correspondent was relaxing near the drinks area. I popped over and he smiled as he recognised the slightly older coach. We reminisced about the Oxford days and the challenges for the British Lions and went on our separate ways. I am delighted that Stuart, has written the foreword to this book. He is an incisive journalist, who is not afraid to tackle controversial topics in rugby, as he did in most topics in his undergraduate days.

It was again during the 2003 Rugby World Cup that I introduced myself to another wonderful man. Wales had just been beaten in a pulsating quarter-final game in Brisbane by England. On the flight back to Sydney I say this powerful looking bearded man strolling down the aircraft isle, so I got to introduce myself to the great Ray Gravelle. What a charming and engaging personality, We spoke for a considerable time about the challenges and strengths of Welsh rugby. It was a great pleasure for me to meet such a humble and passionate Welshman.

We were on a family holiday In the North Devon resort of Woolacombe and enjoying some beach football when I spotted the Sunday Times chief rugby writer Stephen Jones playing with his sons in a nearby game. I have known Stephen for some time in his capacity as rugby writer, and we crossed paths on many occasions. Stephen was brought up in the village of Rogerstone not more than three miles from my home in Risca. Our conversation that day was more about how much our grass roots upbringing had influenced our future careers. Funnily enough, rugby happened to be at the centre of the conversation. A chance meeting on a rather breezy Devon holiday, resort put both of us in reminiscing mode.

OURFC U21S AND KINGHAM HILL SCHOOL

'Rugger – Do It This Way' – Published 1945
'Halves, of course must go on assiduously practising together, experimenting, getting to know each other. Let them and all players "fool about" with the ball a bit during practices, on their own.
They learn much that way'
Mark Sugden and Gerry Hollis

In 2010, Tim Stevens the OURFC administrator, invited me to coach the university's U21 team. The young coaches in situ, both former students of the university, Matt Street and Dom Alonzi, were both promising and diligent. I was reluctant to replace Matt as lead coach. Part of my role was to help the coaches in their development and apply the coaching concepts in which I believed. This age group would be an exciting group to coach. The players had not yet adopted the characteristically physical approach to the game. They had a reasonable skill set, as a result of playing rugby at school. I made it clear to both coaches that I wanted to help, by familiarising them with coaching through a games-based approach. The relationship proved to be very beneficial to me, as both had sound knowledge of the game. Matt, being a specialist forwards coach, was important for our set piece work. Dom possessed excellent organisational and people skills. Both kept me on the right track, monitoring my timekeeping and excessive enthusiasm.

Matt had already arranged a pre-season four-day camp. As I was not working full-time, I was able to attend all sessions. Matt and Dom worked in the academic side of the university, as tutors at Magdalen College. The U21s, under the captaincy of Lewis Roberts, a genial Welshman, had been elected by the players in the squad. The coaching journey began. It was not easy to change players' habits of generally hitting up through contact with the defence. It was equally difficult trying to get players to open up space in the defence, in order to penetrate. In any training, stoppages of play through contact were minimal, a term we might call 'the life of the ball'. There would be a greater emphasis on continuity in play. Fitness levels tend to increase with fewer stoppages in play. We encouraged the players to keep playing through introducing a second ball. In each of the five seasons I worked with the U21s, the pattern of learning appeared to be very similar. I tried to keep the prime concept, of going forward with close support of the ball, central to the teaching. I varied the positions of attack and defence and began all practices in movement. As a result, the players encountered starting positions in which they were both unfamiliar and often uncomfortable. Players were used to starting in linear positions and being static. The introduction of the ball severely tested their adjustment to the ever-changing situations created by the 'game in movement'. Immediate results rarely happen. The learning was not linear. Players learned in varying time scales, according to how rapidly their tactical game and skill levels progressed. The more structured their previous coaching, the longer this process would take. Time was not on our side. Around 60 hours of coaching time was available before the Varsity game. Perhaps I was over estimating my ability to coach such a bright group of young players within this limited timescale. I still had to find, quickly, those practices that would help their tactical understanding. Sometimes, it was a question of trial and error. I always encouraged younger coaches, experiencing problems, to revert to the principles of play. My objectives were 'to go forward and support'.

The pattern of coaching over the five years was relatively similar. I found that, after thirty hours of coaching, the majority of players grasped the concepts. The problems occurred in the matches when the lack of first phase possession, meant fewer opportunities to pressure the opposition with our more continuous game. Perhaps, some key players would make poor choices of play and kick inaccurately, and skill levels would drop under pressure. No side can play without the ball. Matt did a very fine job with set pieces, with his detailed work on scrum and lineout. However, on occasions, against the more physical academy teams, our possession was minimal. The team would have short periods keeping possession during which they played efficiently, through linking and penetrating attacks. Unfortunately, error-stricken periods of play would often follow, because poor choices of play and execution of skills resulted in loss of possession. These proved frustrating for coach and players alike.

As coaches we tried various game practices. These included: ball carriers moving defenders off line; immediate support of the ball after passing, to ensure more choice of support for the new ball carrier; lateral movement by the ball carrier to drag defenders off line. The roll of deep support around the ball carrier was crucial for more effective penetration of the defence. We always tried to encourage the players to apply them in the game play that followed. Even then, not all the learning was linear. When errors occurred in game practice, we would immediately introduce a second ball to ensure stoppages of play were minimal. Frequently, I would slow the practice down while the fundamental learning was taking place. Eventually, though, we needed to play as near to game speed as possible to match a real game.

OURFC U21s lost the first Varsity game by 24 to 5. This does not sound like a success. Oxford made three times as many line breaks as Cambridge but only finished one with a try. The pressure of the big game, coupled with the team having to learn and adjust to a different way of playing, had an adverse effect on the performance. As coaches, we had to look at what took place and find ways to accelerate the learning process. In game-based coaching, the tactical choices are considerable. Although similar in their concepts, each situation is never exactly the same. Success tends to come when the groups of players begin to 'read' the situations in the same way. A term we might call 'reading the game in the same way.'

In our second year with the U21s, it helped that more than half of the squad were returning with sixty hours of coaching already in the bank. We were not starting from such a low base of understanding the game's principles. The role of captain in the squad was very important. He would become a key player in ensuring we persevered with the game style during any difficult times. The captain would feed back the concerns of the team to the coaches. The captain in this new group was Will Fell a second row forward. He was supportive about the team playing how they trained. He understood the methodology of the game.

The pattern of the previous year's progress was similar in the early games. However, the difference made by a four-day pre-season camp and a more solid foundation of how to play meant there were longer periods of effective penetration and support of the ball. One major problem was to improve players' skills, especially the handling in and around contact. The other major challenge for the players was decision-making after initial penetration of the first line of defence. All too frequently, both ball-carrier and support players made ineffective choices of play. As coaches, we designed practices to play against layered forms of defence. There were frequent stoppages of play as the players wrestled with trying to find solutions to maintain continuity of the game. Nevertheless, the improvement in game understanding came slightly earlier, around three weeks before the Varsity game. The players benefited from the training that concentrated on playing on the long axis of the field, with closer and deep support. They became more proficient in transferring the ball to the wide axis, where space appeared. The final game before the Varsity match, against Esher Academy, produced the most fluid and effective rugby of the term. The team now believed that they could play rugby against Cambridge in the style that had underpinned their coaching all term. The big question was 'Can we produce the same rugby under the bigger pressure of the Varsity game?'

The requirement to play more rugby with ball in hand had the desired effect in that game. One of the best tries I have seen scored, at any level, gave the team the greatest satisfaction. It started five metres from our line with a turnover, in a tackle secured by Barnes, the hooker. We moved the ball immediately across the width of the field near to our own posts. Cambridge expected a kick. From his position on the wide axis, our wing 'Sonny Bill' Williams (not the current All Black) ran to the halfway line, where a cover tackle occurred. Quick possession and penetration by the captain and No.8, Tom Reeson-Price, followed on the narrow side. Another quick ruck on the 22-line led to a dummy break by fly-half Dace against a disorganised defence. Then came a transfer to the player who won the original turnover, Barnes, in close support, who scored by the posts. This memorable try involved over half the team and covered the length of the field. To cap the day, Dean Irvine the loose head prop intercepted a pass on his own goal line and sprinted the length of the field to score. What a tale he has to tell his grandchildren, of his big day at Twickenham.

The next season was under the captaincy of Chris O'Halloran. He was a full back who encouraged the side to play the same style of game. OURFC U21s lost the Varsity match. The inaccuracy of the handling and a debilitating hamstring injury to Chris seemed to affect the team's performance. I needed to address some issues of improving the skills under pressure and help the players find better tactical choices when slow ball occurs.

The final year of the U21s Varsity match followed. The captain was a second row forward, Henry Wetheraldt. He proved to be a pivotal figure in the preparation for the Twickenham game. Key players at numbers 2, 8, 9, 10 and 15 played a major role in a significant win. That game saw the most comprehensive victory and performance of all the years I coached the U21s. The Whippets, a second string U21s, mostly made up of freshers, were the first to play at Iffley Road, a week before the first team played. The stunning 52 –10 victory over their Cambridge counterparts, contained eight tries, seven of which started well inside our own half. The running lines of ball carriers, support play and option choosing were of a level I had not seen before with this age group. Cambridge played a more structured game in which kicking and one-out passing from contact were dominant. Our set pieces, under Matt Street's guidance, meant more and better first-phase ball. The stand out performer for the Whippets was Ed David, an electric runner with an acute sense of game understanding. Ed was elected the OURFC captain for 2019. The side came to Twickenham with a heightened sense of what they wanted to achieve. The captain had asked me if he could run two coaching sessions without the coaches. Of course, as coaches we agreed. I gather from conversations with players later that they had frank discussions about some issues. However, at the finish, Henry told them that we play how we train. They also asked me to conduct the U21s choir, singing outside Christ Church College, a few days before the game. I still wonder whether my choral skills were a better trump card than my coaching. Direct from the kick off, the team tried to exit their 22 area by passing and running. It took five minutes to get out of the 22 but the ball was never dropped. The confidence they built from that period grew during the game. They won 32 -10. It was pleasing to watch the variety

of ways they attacked. Sometimes they made ground by penetrating in close forma-
tion through evasion and off-loading. At other times, they spread the ball wide, after
committing defenders to the contact areas. Ed David, a sub, scored a sixty metre try.

My time with the U21s, ably supported by Matt Street and Dom Alonzi the manager, was one of the most stimulating and rewarding periods I have had in coaching.

The universities of Oxford and Cambridge decided, regrettably in my view, to
change their format of age group rugby. They established an U20 format but with
no Varsity game at Twickenham. The U20s match between Oxford and Cambridge
match would now take place in the less congested, second term. I think a good exposure for the undergraduate game could be as a curtain-raiser game at a premier-
ship ground. The Women's Varsity game replaced the U21 game on the morning
of the men's Varsity game. This is an important advance for the development of
women's student rugby.

Comments made by the U21s of their experiences in their time with OURFC:
Ed David U21 – Player – OURFC Captain 2019

'The coaching method was less prescriptive than that I had experienced in recent years and unlike anything I had come across at school.

'We were not limited to playing what was in front of us, a phrase that is overused
in rugby and which implies that a simple glance at a static defensive line should
determine your next move. Rather, we were encouraged to fully exploit any space
we had created – by playing close attention to the body language of defenders and
manipulating the opposition accordingly. I fondly remember the frustration of the
coaching team when we failed to take the opportunities these offered us. Another
benefit of this method is that it is not specific to forward or back play and places a
strong emphasis on good basic skills.'

KINGHAM HILL SCHOOL

During the summer following my last U21 Varsity game, the head of rugby
at Kingham Hill School, a small independent school situated in idyllic surroundings near Chipping Norton in the Cotswolds, asked me to coach the senior rugby
squad. The time commitment would entail two coaching sessions and a midweek
game during the autumn term. Kingham's rugby fixture list entailed matches mainly against independent schools of a similar size. The list included occasional fixtures against second teams of larger independent schools. The head of rugby, Chris
Ashton, (not the England wing), had a desire to improve the coaching available to
the boys. I was to discover another challenge for my development as a coach. The
school nestles on a hill. It has stunning panoramic views of the surrounding coun-

tryside and looks down on the town of Chipping Norton. Two rugby pitches occupy a relatively sheltered area, overlooked by the school chapel at one end. A quaint, small, wooden changing room is at the other end. The arrangement was to carry out a four-day pre-season training course. Abilities in the squad ranged from a couple of county-level players to a larger group of relative novices, including players who had never played the game. All of these players came from countries not recognised as leading rugby nations. Among the nationalities represented were Ukrainians, Russians, Chinese, Spanish, Columbian, Thai and American. Some of these players went on to make remarkable progress. They became very adept at the game, after just a couple of months of coaching and playing. Their previous coaching had entailed mostly structured, drill-like activities. In this pre-season camp, organised by Chris, we were able to introduce the game-based coaching process with some intensity. The boys responded well to the processes we used. Those new to the game were able to understand the game's complexities much sooner than those used to a more drill-based method.

As with all the other teams I coached, the familiarity with learning through

Enjoying the company of the senior students of Kingham Hill rugby team who celebrated an outstanding season of flowing rugby.

playing in game situations took time. One dominant player, Tom Rolf, a particularly athletic and skilled flanker, stood out from the rest of the players. There are huge benefits to have such a player. However, among a group of such a range of ability, this could present a challenge for less experienced players not to 'hide' in the

Coaching at Kingham Hill School

player in far more decision-making opportunities.

The next three seasons saw a number of changes take place. The school arranged fixtures against stronger, rugby playing established independent schools such as Stowe, Royal Latin in Bucks, and Magdalen College School, Oxford. These games, against the second XVs, replaced the games against the similarly sized schools, who found the gap in playing standards increasing as Kingham's standards of play improved. Kingham experienced the same problem as the greater experience and expertise of the established schools proved difficult to overcome.

On the plus side, more players attended rugby training. For the first time, a number of third team fixtures were arranged to give these new players a chance to play matches. In summary, the standard of play would improve if it were possible to train the rugby coaches at all the ages before senior level. Over recent seasons Joe Winpenny worked with the U15 group, and hopefully, this can begin next year with the U14s.

During 2019, I began in-service coaching with the teachers who were involved with the sides in the junior part of the school. If the coaching process can be started when the players arrive at Kingham, then the benefits of game understanding should be accelerated by the time they reach the upper school. A new impetus and energy was provided by head of senior rugby Tom Phillips. He recognised the impact the coaching was having on individual player development, as well as an improvement of game understanding.

Me and the boys at Kingham Hill School

During the 2019 season we began to see the benefits of the coaching in players tactical understanding of the game, as a result of more players having experienced the training for more than two years. More of the senior players and some of the more inexperienced players, are contributing more constructively to the coaching programme. They ask more pertinent and relevant questions, and are not afraid to ask me how some of the practices we do are relevant to the game. It makes me look carefully at what practices I am providing. The last fifteen minutes of the 2019 season in a game against Bloxham school, saw the team provide the best examples of sustained penetrating, supporting, dynamic, and innovative rugby I have witnessed, from any team I have had the privilege of coaching. What a glorious way for both the team and the coaches to end a season!

For me, the experience of coaching a group of players with such a range of experience in rugby was very new. I suppose the exposure to the game for players with little or no experience is one that only more time for practice can solve. The physical differences between teams are much more difficult to resolve. The 2019 Japanese side seems to have found some answers to the great physical challenges facing them. Make fewer contacts!

The autumn term of 2021 gave me the opportunity to work with the coaches and players in the under 12, 14 and 15 age groups. The initial coaching sessions were encouraging. Over a six week period, the coaches revealed the players had made incredible strides in their understanding and application of the 'movement game'.

Schools they played in the early term scored easy victories. In the last weeks of term, return fixtures resulted in Kingham Hill teams matching the more direct play of their opponents with well constructed tries, effective passing and support play.

OXFORD U21S SQUAD
'OPEN HOUSE' COMMENTS

Introduction

This report is a compilation of oral interviews, conducted in February 2015, with seven players who were part of the 2014/15 OURFC U21 team. The focal point of that team's season was the annual varsity match against Cambridge University's U21 team. This match took place at Twickenham on the 11th December 2014. The Oxford team won by a score of 36 points to 12. These interviews were an attempt to understand, from the players' perspective, why the culture of rugby of the Oxford U21's set-up was successful.

The seven players consisted of one front-row, one second-row, two back-rows, one centre and two back-three players. They had different levels of experience. Three had played in previous seasons for the U21s, and so were senior players. Four were newcomers to the U21s in the 2014/15 season. They were all asked the same questions and their answers were recorded electronically. A summary of their responses follows.

What is the style of rugby which the U21s try to play?

While the exact definitions varied slightly from player to player, there was an overwhelming consensus about the philosophy of rugby of the Oxford U21s "It's about moving players and creating space rather than bashing through walls of players, trying to make small yardage. We believe we can play anywhere. Every possession is an opportunity to create space and put someone through that space. It's much more about teamwork and creating space than individual brilliance." One player said: "It's about ball-playing, trying to get everyone involved. The different positions don't have such structured roles. We're focused on reacting to what the other team are doing in defence rather than creating set phases such as 'going through the centres three times then going right'." Another player stated "It's all about the penetration game. It involves free-flowing, attacking skill, where everyone on the team has the confidence to run with the ball and develop space." The players seemed to agree that the philosophy was about 'trying to play behind a defence as opposed to in front of them, trying to use the space behind them instead of running at them.' Another player thought that the game style involved "moving the ball quickly, trying to make an initial line break and then ensuring that you have the support to offload when it's on. When we do go through the phases, it's usually to facilitate space out wide, which we then utilise. We're not trying to arm-wrestle the opposition."

Is this philosophy effective, and what does it offer as opposed to other styles of playing rugby?

While the players offered considered answers, recognising the fact that "no style is perfect", there was also a general consensus that the U21s style was highly effective. In response to the question, one player (a newcomer to the team in 2014/15 and one who was, by his own admission, sceptical about the style of play for much of the season) answered: "Absolutely. It is perhaps difficult to play it, if you're new to it, but it is much, much more difficult to defend it. It offers variety, freedom to play, and problems for defenders." A back-row player offered: "It definitely gives you an edge, especially when you're trying to play a team who outweigh you or are more physical than you are. We played teams like the Bedford Blues' Academy, and if you tried to take them head-on, you'd get battered. This approach to rugby negates differences in physicality." One of the back-three players said that in his previous experience of playing rugby he had always felt a considerable pressure to be constantly aware of field position, which constrained his judgement about whether he should kick or run with the ball. He then said that the penetration-style game is "quite liberating. If it's on, you can give it a go, and not worry about field position or fear that any mistake you make will be fatal. Sometimes, in rugby, you can worry too much about what you're doing wrong, rather than what you're doing right. So, it's nice to have the freedom to do what you want to do." One player saw touch rugby sessions against the full university side as evidence of the style's effectiveness: "We played the Blues at touch rugby. They were much quicker than us, but they were much worse at creating and using space."

Most of the players thought that this style could transfer to other rugby environments. One player thought that other teams probably would adopt the penetration style more effectively.

This is counterproductive, because we're all intelligent and like to think things through, so everyone has their own opinions. We should have just shut up and got on with doing what we were told. This was particularly true for the lineout but there were similar issues in training our attacking play. It is a very simple way of playing rugby, and the more you embrace that the easier it is to play. We didn't have an especially talented group of players, or one which was particularly suited to that way of playing, so anyone could have done it. This showed against Cambridge, who had a similar group of players to us, but we won because our game plan was vastly better to theirs, even though they were as good as us individually."

Two players thought that the reason that the style was so effective was that there is more space available at U21 level because players are smaller than, and physically inferior to, those at higher levels. They thought that teams with better defensive organisation might be able to cope with the penetration-style, and so it might not be effective at a higher level. However, one of them also made the point that: "I could see it probably working (with a professional side), because the fundamentals (such as keeping people honest and narrow then exploiting space) stay the same."

Despite this slight uncertainty about how transferable the penetration style is, the dominant feeling was that it had something to offer every team. "Playing the penetration game gives you the confidence that you have this definite philosophy and way of playing that everyone knows. It can be the focus of team talks, players chatting after the game, discussing training, and so on. It gives you a feeling of being set apart from the opposition. You feel that you can turn up to an opposition that might fancy beating you, but you can have the confidence that you can beat them with this way of playing. It represents something tangible that you can think about and improve rather than just getting lost in vague thoughts about rugby as a whole."

What is necessary for this style to be effective?

The single factor overwhelmingly cited by the interviewees as responsible for the success of this style was belief on the part of the players. "The players must believe in it. If people pretend to believe, and try to look like they're playing it, it won't work. They need to buy into it absolutely. One person going off with a different agenda wrecks it for the team. Everyone needs to be on the same page. People must have good hands, be intelligent in setting depth of support, etc. There is so much freedom and flexibility on offer through this style, but players have to take it."

One player said, "Right up until the last couple of games before the Varsity match, we didn't flourish with this style because people didn't fully invest themselves into the penetration game. They were stuck in their old ways, which I was guilty of as well, and it took me a while to get into it."

Another player, asked to explain why he was deeply sceptical of the penetration game until very late on in the season, answered: "I thought it sounded too good to be true. I couldn't understand how something so minor could be so effective. It seemed like something that forwards would do in loose play and that would be it. Backs tend to overcomplicate things, thinking that you have to throw elaborate miss-passes and run dummy lines, etc, especially playing at this level where you want to prove yourself by doing complicated things." When asked what changed his mind, it was "seeing it happen in a game against Esher. I'd seen it in video sessions, but actually being in a match situation and seeing it work was what convinced me." All the players interviewed seemed to share this experience of being deeply sceptical before seeing the penetration-style work in training and actual match-play. From which point onwards they bought into the style.

One player cited a number of skills which players who wanted to play this system needed to develop: "Learning when to give the pass and when to keep it. You need to learn to assess space, keep head up, be constantly looking around, looking for space, defence, support, etc. You need to learn to run at the inside shoulder of the defence to open space out wide. Depth of support is particularly important. Opening defenders is dependent on fine margins and tiny steps by the attacking players, so subtle adjustments are necessary. A good level of handling skill is necessary. You need better fitness, and it seems particularly hard for forwards, going from one side of the pitch to the other and not knowing where the ball is going to go next. There were a number of changes which people needed to make to their natural style of play in order to penetrate successfully. It's difficult to learn when to offload and when passing in contact would just be throwing the ball around willy-nilly."

Another commented, "You need to modify the expectation that you can only do stuff to influence the game when you have the ball. You can be doing stuff off the ball, for instance, setting up support lines of running. It is quite difficult to get into the expectation that you will be running and supporting from anywhere." The players acknowledged that the penetration game was radically different to anything else they had been coached. The centre said: "I'm used to a more direct style of rugby, using my size and speed to take people on. The idea of slowing down and trying to move people around was extremely unfamiliar to me, challenging and frustrating."

One of the front-row players said: "I'm more accustomed to the meathead approach to rugby, so it was difficult to get out of that mode and into thinking 'I should be here, I should be supporting, I should be making space for someone else. Conceptually, it is not a difficult style to understand, but I found it difficult to carry out. Translating the style into reality was difficult, but that's the same for everyone. Once you embrace it, it all comes together. It took a few weeks for it to come together, only happened really after about seven weeks of coaching, and before that we were disjointed." At the other end of the spectrum, a back-three player commented that: "I found it really difficult being told to slow down. I didn't understand why the coaches were telling me that. I was the number one try-scorer at school, and it was the same with college rugby, where I would just go the length of the pitch and score, so I was not looking for support because I had the ability. This pre-season (2014), I focused on exactly what I was being asked to do, which was to make a break, slow down, and try to look for support. Other players who were in a similar position to me just tried to run, and they got tackled and turned over. They need to learn something that seems massively counterintuitive, which you can only understand when you see it work. Some very talented players find the penetration game ridiculous. One example is being told to slow down before contact in some situations, where the usual assumption is that you should take the contact and try to get on the front foot. Each player needs to have a personal realisation of being open to being taught these things, especially props!"

What did you think of the way it was coached?

As the main figure in the coaching of the penetration-oriented style of rugby, Lynn Evans was, unsurprisingly, the focus of the players' comments on the U21 coaching set-up. "Lynn's penetration game is confusing when you first play it. It takes a few weeks to understand. Of course, there was a huge squad of about seventy at the beginning of the season, so it was difficult for coaches."

Another player thought that "The way the attacking game is coached is very effective. I like that we play lots of open games, where the coaches just chuck the ball to someone and expect something to happen. That epitomises the style of the U21s, being able to play anywhere on the pitch in whatever situation, which teams don't expect." A player who had been on the team's pre-season camp said: "The penetration style needs to be taught from day one. There was a lot of dissent on pre-season because everyone was like, 'What the hell are we doing?' We were just running around every day with the ball playing the penetration game for hours, but this was definitely important to make it effective."

One player who was new to the U21s in 2014/15 commented that "The video analysis sessions were really good. Touch was particularly effective as well. Everybody was together in one place, where normally teams split into forwards and backs. It mixed people up and allowed people to see that wherever you were on the pitch, if you did these simple things, it would come off. It took a long time for people to buy into the idea and understand what Lynn was driving at. *Touch rugby is the only effective way of learning how to manipulate players in a game-realistic situation. Lots of players were frustrated initially and were trying to do what came instinctively to them, such as trying to make a break on the outside or going around people or just running at people. There was a switch around two weeks before Varsity, where people bought into the idea and saw that it was effective. I was sceptical at the beginning because I was playing touch all the time, the way I would normally do it and getting frustrated and getting an earful from Lynn. However, there were a few players who were experienced and respected Lynn enough to take his ideas on board, and once they took the lead everyone else followed."

*It was not touch rugby that we played but a co-operative game of block and hold by the defence to help the attackers understand the concepts of the playing method. Lynn

All the interviewees commented that the philosophy took a while to take hold in the team. Later on in the season, "Even the 21s weren't really getting it, and then in the last two weeks of the season we developed a drill where five people attack two defenders down a line. This is where things clicked." Another player agreed: "In terms of when things clicked for us, I think of a particular Saturday morning training session which replaced a cancelled game. Lynn did a drill in the dead ball area, where five attackers just ran at two defenders, giving it to the next bloke, five times. Because it was such a small space, the attackers had to draw the defenders perfectly, and support runners had to line up right. We did the drill that morning for a long time without doing it well, but once it clicked it was 'Oh, that's really simple', and you can do it anywhere on the pitch. And once you're through the defence, you have so much space to run into. People who had done that drill were much better at the penetration game than the people who came into it in the next week. Once that drill happened, the click happened."

One senior player saw an advantage of using the penetration system from a coach's perspective. "When it wasn't working, you could strip everything else away and focus on one little thing – penetration. Being able to focus like this really changed things when we went back to gameplay." The coaches were able to target their coaching as a result of this style of game play, but the players also noted that the personality of the coaches was important. "I thought that there was a significant change between 2013 and 2014. Last year the coaches were harder to talk to. This year they seemed more relaxed, chilled out and approachable this year. They seemed to be seeing players as people rather than just seeing them as means of fulfilling their goals." Another interviewee saw the importance of off-field coaching: "People were able to sit with Lynn and ask questions in classroom sessions. This was particularly helpful, especially towards the end of the process, once people had got a good handle on things. People were then able to walk away from the classroom and get things done on the pitch."

What could have been done better?'

"Sometimes it is difficult to understand Lynn. He has all his ideas in his head, but perhaps struggles to express those ideas clearly, and sometimes a younger player in his first session might not get it. However, his ideas are absolutely brilliant, and a few weeks of being coached by him make anyone on the pitch a better player, without a doubt. It is good to have another person to handle the nitty-gritty of defence, forward-work, etc, which Lynn doesn't seem to be so keen on."

Some players pointed out specific areas which they thought the 21s had to ignore for the sake of implementing the penetration game. "We perhaps compromised on set piece defence, but we had to spend the time on the penetration game. We had very poor set-piece defence in the backs, which is very nice, but we never covered it."

However, the same player recognised that, "We do more penetration game than other stuff, but it took us a while to get it. It is a challenging thing to implement, so you have to spend the necessary time on it." A couple of players thought that "drills to supplement the penetration game early on would have helped players who were struggling", and "perhaps more three-on-twos would have been good, where you slow it down, even walk it through to begin with."

One player commented that, "It was good that everyone's voice was heard, and perhaps you were able to pick up on common things which everyone was finding difficult. However, it was sometimes frustrating because there were too many voices. Senior players need to demand silence from people. Having too many opinions can be confusing. Some of the chat was just trying to give off the impression that you knew what you were talking about and were trying to give that impression to the coaches with an eye on selection."

Another player thought that it seemed "quite tough for talented young players to break into the team, partly because of how difficult it is to fit into a team who has been playing this way for some time. The only way to get used to the system is to play it, so if you're not getting game time then it's difficult to get good, but not being good at the system means you don't get game time." The player recognised, however, that this was perhaps an unavoidable difficulty.

One senior player thought that "You do need a mix between offence and defence. Doing the penetration game all the time can lead to a lack of progress, because, over time, people just get stuck in their ways, making the same mistakes again and again. You need to stop, do something else, then come back and try to figure out how to do things differently." Another player suggested that this "could have been done with more frequent short classroom sessions interspersed with play on the field. The coaches could be trying to inculcate principles in the classroom and then give players an immediate opportunity to put them into practice, before going back to the classroom to discuss what could be done better."

In terms of the coaching, the players thought that "continuity was sometimes an issue especially with Streety and Ben (both coaches) coaching slightly different things in defence. We would often have either Streety or Ben, and they had different opinions on lineouts, driving mauls, etc, so difficult to get a go-forward. We did a lot of lineouts, but because of inconsistent instructions it was difficult to know what you were doing when. Streety's up-and-out defence was not quite the same as Ben's defence, and there were differences in breakdown coaching." However, nearly all the interviewees thought that there was impressive uniformity in the vision of the coaches for the attacking philosophy of the team, and that this uniformity was the only way that the penetration-game could be implemented effectively.

Another suggestion for improvement to the coaching lay in the area of coaches offering individual feedback. Though the players who suggested this all recognised the difficulties of offering personalised feedback when coaching an enormous squad. "The coaches seemed hesitant to give much feedback, and it was difficult to know where you stood in the squad until a few days before Varsity. There was not much continuity in training before the Whippets Varsity (on the 2nd December 2014). Coaches could be more open about where you stood in the squad and give you more feedback about how you could improve. I felt out in the woods, not knowing which team I was playing for and how I'd been doing. Having said that, I love the rugby and I love the atmosphere here. It is very progress orientated. Maybe more feedback from the coaches would have meant that talent didn't fall by the wayside. Sometimes you're just going through the motions and don't really see yourself improving, so feedback would help for that player's development. Focused coaching would have helped, especially with this style of play. It is extremely valuable to take someone aside and say, 'This is what you're doing, so try this.'"

It is revealing to see how players perceive coaching that has less structure than most coaching sessions they have experienced. Structure of course has its place in coaching, and many players feel more comfortable having responsibility for their actions taken away by the coach Lynn.

Conclusion

The players' sentiment can be summed-up best in the following quotation: "I actually feel quite privileged to have been part of this culture of rugby. We were taking on academies aiming at producing professional players, and it was a little bit embarrassing that we were on the pitch with them as individuals. Our ability to be competitive in those games was only possible because of the way we play. This ultimately showed in the Varsity game, where Cambridge lacked ideas. It was really enjoyable, by far the most enjoyable rugby experiences I've ever had." The experiences reported by the players seem to suggest that the philosophy of rugby of the U21's coaches offers a radically new style of rugby, one that is simultaneously effective and personally-rewarding. It allows the players who take part in it to develop creativity in their rugby that will lead to intense enjoyment and fulfilment, at whatever level they play. It is also remarkably effective. Because most players quickly become accustomed to having to solve problems on their own, without resorting to coaching guidance, they are well prepared for match situations. They are able to adapt to their opposition and try to find a means of scoring. It is a style which all rugby teams should explore, at the very least.

REFLECTION

'He was not of the most common mould of rugby men. He was the philosopher king of the rugby world. As a coach he tried at times to persuade and convince in the most astute and democratic fashion. On other occasions he guided, as all the best teachers do, in such a way that the player, like the fortunate pupil, would be surprised to find a wonderful discovery for himself. Since the discovery is your own, or appears to be so, the reward is that much sweeter and infinitely satisfying. The glory was his as it was ours. The twain, player and coach, meet in glorious harmony.'

Gerald Davies – Wales and British Lions on his coach Carwyn James after the Lions Tour of New Zealand 1971

Can I be certain? Was it in those carefree days of my early years and my youth that this freedom to play, uninhibited by adult intervention, fired my love of sport and play?

Growing up in my Welsh valley town, sometimes, I was Bleddyn Williams, prince of Welsh centres, jinking my way through a spread-eagled English defence. At other times, I was Ivor Allchurch, a visionary inside forward of the 1950s and a Welsh football legend. My educated left foot was making his slide-rule passes. In the summer, I became Don Shepherd, the cunning Glamorgan off-spinner, bamboozling the powerful South African touring cricketers at Swansea. I lived and breathed sport, whether at school or in my spare time.

Rarely did I enjoy the powerful and fiery contests. The more aesthetic aspects of sport had a greater appeal for me. It was a thrill for me to watch many threequarters in Welsh rugby using their guile, their deceptive skills of dummying, sidestepping and an elegant kicking game. In cricket, watching the elegant batting of the England batsman Reg Simpson, I gained the greatest pleasure from his leg glance, cover drive and the late cut.

I saw sport as a vehicle to give me release from the ardours of studying. Schoolwork and college work interfered with my sport. I did just enough to get by, passing examinations with nothing to spare. A life in sport was all I wanted. My choice, in those days, was between doing physical training in the military or joining the teaching profession. My National Service was compulsory, but I did not dislike that two-year period. However, I wanted to work with young people.

Discovering and developing my game knowledge and my skills at many and varied types of sport, stimulated me to pursue a life consumed by activities. My mother always encouraged me to play sports. She had a huge influence in guiding me towards a sporting career. She often used the phrase 'Lynn have you got ants in your pants?' For my part, I had a long-standing, personal desire to become a teacher.

My family has always been supportive of my rugby. We are a sporting family. My wife Mary has had a life in tennis administration, at the top echelons of the

My close family
Left to right Me, Dougie, Cal, Karey, Rory, Cressida, Iain, Cam and Mary

Lawn Tennis Association. Mary is, also, a fanatical rugby supporter both of Exeter Chiefs and England. Her critique of rugby refereeing is legendary in our family. We watch separate TVs at home for England v Wales internationals! My two daughters enjoy sports. Karey is a tennis player and elegant skier and her husband, Calum, is a top skier. While at Oxford University, Cressida gained netball and tennis blues and her husband, Iain, gained cricket and golf blues, and played against the Australian cricket tourists. Grandson Cameron has been my interpreter, on coaching courses in France and Italy. Grandson Rory has started his rugby coaching awards at the tender age of twenty-one, and has aspirations to be involved in acting. Dougie, our youngest grandson, is both autistic and amazing. He plays the piano, though he cannot read music. He plays by ear. His rendition of Sospan Fach is truly moving for his grandfather. If anyone needs cheering up, Dougie is the tonic required. He is the only table tennis player I know who tells himself a story while actually playing!

My brother Alan, who died in 2017, was a close and supportive figure in my life. He married his childhood girlfriend from Crosskeys, Janet Lewis .He loved rugby and was noted for his intelligence when playing the game. The passion for his beloved Wales was evident in Paris, following a Welsh win against France. While going up to his hotel room, in the lift, he suddenly cried out, 'Great!'. He threw his fist in the air and smashed out the light. Welsh passion knows no bounds.

As you see from the book, I continued to explore the opportunities sport provided for progressing my life. I did not want the administrative burdens required for deputy-headships and beyond.

Key figures in my working life encouraged me to explore and develop my thinking and my career. Ben Halliday, a wonderful headteacher and man, encouraged me to expand my sporting interests while I taught at his new school at Littlemore. He gave me the outstanding support that every inexperienced young teacher needed. At the school, we played over fifteen different sports. For some sports I needed to gain more education. This was not a burden, but an opportunity to increase my all-round knowledge of sport. Brian Poxon, a local teacher and rugby administrator gave me chances to coach at regional level. He provided great support for my early development as a coach.

A significant breakthrough occurred for me, when the RFU began coaching courses, especially for teachers. Their technical director, Don Rutherford, encouraged me to gain more and more knowledge and expertise in rugby coaching, through linking me with experienced coaches.

Playing rugby at county level enabled me to experience the game at the top level. Oxfordshire were very competitive and frequently won the Southern Group, under the direction of the forward-thinking Geoff Windsor-Lewis.

I was extremely fortunate to meet and liaise with two exceptional and visionary coaches of world class level, H.V. 'Chalky' White and Pierre Villepreux. They shared their knowledge and encouraged me to extend mine. They taught me to think creatively and to pay close attention to detail in the game. Such coaches are rare. I tried to follow their example and aimed to share my coaching knowledge, in whatever way possible, with any aspiring coach.

In 2011, the RFU honoured me with a Lifetime Award for Coaching Excellence. I received this alongside another special coaching friend of mine, Albi Thomas, a true man of Cornwall. This award marked over fifty years of coaching my beloved sport of rugby union. I was most grateful and humbled to receive this award.

My journey has been a long one, with many special experiences along the way. There were obstacles and some testing moments. However, the destination, hopefully not quite finished, has made it all worthwhile. There are no other words than a passion and love of the game that continue to drive me on. Working with young players and coaches, at Littlemore and Kingham, continues to give me the desire to give something back to the game. After all these years, I remain convinced that the best and most enjoyable way to play the game, for the benefit of coaches, players and spectators is through the philosophy of 'le Plaisir du Mouvement(PDM)'.

One of the great challenges facing the coach using a player- centred style of coaching is to resist the temptation to jump in with comments, when some parts of the coaching are not going well. Indeed, one of the benefits of this style gives players more opportunities to be free from restraints-led coaching. It is beneficial for the player to fail sometimes and to evaluate the reasons. Being patient, as a player-centred coach, is beneficial for the long-term development of the players.

I was fortunate, early in my teaching career, to attend a coaching course for teachers led by Rod Thorpe. He was one of the TGFU pioneers and a lecturer at Loughborough College, at the time, a teacher training institution. The course looked at the principles of the use of games to aid game understanding. The training PE teachers experienced in the sixties and seventies, used the method of warm up followed by skills training and, if necessary, unit skills, finishing with a game. Experiments at Loughborough had convinced Rod that this structured approach was not the most effective way to help players with the complex tactical challenges of games. Using the game as a motivating tool, while learning how and where the skills fit into the game, provides a more enjoyable experience for the athlete. There is a place for a more didactic style of coaching, but this should occur sparingly. The better learning experience would allow the player to be an active contributor. During a tactically oriented warm up session with12 year-olds, I asked them to devise their own 1 v 1 game. They had to make up the rules, the scoring system and to develop the game as they saw fit. There were more original games than I could possibly have dreamt up.

The foundation of the **PDM** game is tactical priority over technique. The major task, not an easy one, is to ensure the game they play is at the appropriate level. It is important that most of the players understand the objectives and can apply them in the game. The coach, through observation, can either ease the challenges or make them more difficult. There are many stories of top athletes, in all sports, who experienced playing a wide range of sports when they were young. The great tennis player Roger Federer is a fine example. Such increased exposure to tactical challenges, helps the player to realise how many of the actions in the various games are similar. The different sizes, weights, shapes, textures of the implements used in the different games, help the player to develop the appropriate skills, necessary in all of these sports.

The two words 'perception' and 'adaptation' should be emphasised for the coach who wants to develop a player and game-centred approach to coaching. The dictionary meanings for 'adaptation' include modification, change, shift, habituation, remodelling, version and naturalisation. Rick Shuttleworth, an Australian coach working in England, is very knowledgeable about the practical use of adaptability in coaching. You could be in for a long night's conversation with Rick on this topic. 'Perception' is something we must help the player to develop. The dictionary provides some telling vocabulary here: conception, consciousness, discernment, feeling, grasp, idea, impression, insight, notion, observation, recognition, sensation, sense, taste, and understanding. Surely, this is terminology made in heaven for the 'Perceptive Coach'.

RFU PRESIDENT'S VALUE THE VOLUNTEER OUTSTANDING CONTRIBUTION AWARDS 2021

Saturday, 13th November 2021 at Twickenham

Presentation by Nigel Gillingham RFU

Mary and I at the stadium

With the great Australian John Eales at lunch at Twickenham

IN MY LIFETIME

1930s

26th June 1938   *1938 I was born in Tredegar Monmouthshire*

1939   War declared when Germany invaded Poland

1940s

May 1940   Thousands of British troops evacuated from Dunkirk

August 1940   Battle of Britain begins as Luftwaffe attacks Britain

November 1942   Welfare State created in Britain

May 1944   Butler Act creates free Secondary Education in Britain

8th May 1945   Britain celebrates end of the war on Victory in Europe day

1945   United Nations comes into existence with Britain a founder member

29th July 1948   First Olympic Games since WW2 held in London

1949   *I begin Grammar School at Pontroaun in Pontymister*

June 1949   George Orwell publishes Animal Farm

1950s

1951   *I saw my first ever Ballet, Swan Lake*

                                    Festival of Britain opened in London

29th May 1953   Everest conquered Hilary and Tensing first to the top

2nd June 1953   Coronation of Elizabeth II at Westminster Abbey

1st December 1953   Rosa Parks strikes blow for Civil rights by sitting at the front of a bus in American South

1955   Commercial Television first broadcast ITV

1956   *I become a grave digger!*

                                    Called up for National Service in the RAF

October 1956   Britain's first Nuclear Power station opens

November 1956   Britain and France invade Egypt in Suez Canal crisis

1958   *De-mobbed from RAF*

December 1958   First British Motorway opens M6 Preston By-pass

1960s

November 1962   *Married my wife, Mary*

28th November 1962	*Our daughter Karey born*
22nd November 1963	John F Kennedy assassinated in Dallas Texas
15th March 1964	*Our daughter Cressida born*
July 1965	First Comprehensive Schools open in UK
	Death Penalty in UK abolished
July 1966	England win Football World Cup
July 1967	Abortion and homosexuality are legalised
July 20th 1969	American lands first men on the Moon
1970s	
1971	Decimalised currency replaces old Stirling currency
January 1973	Britain joins the EEC
1976	*Founded Littlemore RFC*
1980s	
1980	*Commenced coaching at Oxford University Rugby Club*
	First contact with Pierre Villepreux and a week visit to Toulouse Rugby Club
3rd April 1982	1982 Argentina invade the Falkland Islands
12th March 1984	Miners' strike begins and lasts for over a year
9th November 1989	Fall of the Berlin Wall
1990s	
1990	*Took early retirement from teaching to work for the RFU and Oxford University*
6th May 1992	Channel Tunnel Opens and London and Paris connected by rail
1994	First women priests ordained in Church of England
3rd February 1995	*First grandchild, Cam, born*
1995	Hosts South Africa win Rugby World Cup presented by Nelson Mandela
	World Rugby Union becomes a professional game
22nd November 1996	*Second grandchild, Rory, born*
September 1997	Scotland and Wales vote in favour of devolution
25th January 1995	*Third grandchild, Dougie, born*
10th April 1998	Northern Ireland Assembly established

1999	Rugby World Cup hosted by Wales
2000s	
11th September 2001	9/11 attack on the twin towers in New York
2003	*Retired from RFU*
20th March 2003	Britain joins US forces to invade Iraq
22nd Nov 2003	England win the Rugby World Cup beating hosts Australia in the final
2004	*Started working for the Penguins International Coaching Group*
7th July 2005	7/7/ bombings in London
2007	France hosts Rugby World Cup won by South Africa
2010s	
11th May 2011	Osama Bin Laden killed by US Navy Seal team
2012	Olympic Games hosted by London
	Celebrated our Golden wedding anniversary
	Received a Lifetime Award for services to rugby by RFU
2016	Fiji win the Olympic Rugby Sevens title in Brazil
2021	*RFU President's Value the Volunteer Outstanding Contribution Award*

TESTIMONIALS

Ed David
Former U21 – Player OURFC Captain 2019

The coaching method was less prescriptive than those I had experienced in recent years and was unlike anything I had come across at school.

We were not limited to playing what was in front of us, a phrase that is overused in rugby and which implies that with a simple glance a static defensive line should determine your next move. Rather, we were encouraged to fully exploit any space we had created – by playing close attention to the body language of defenders and manipulating the opposition accordingly. I fondly remember the frustration of the coaching team when we failed to take the opportunities this offered us. Another benefit of this method is that it is not specific to forward or back play and places a strong emphasis on good basic skills.

Tim Stevens
Littlemore RFC
LRFC Player 1984 – 2001. Captain 1996. President 2003 to present

In the summer of 1976, Lynn Evans (Head of PE at, the then, Peers School in Littlemore, Oxford) invited a group of local men to a meeting to discuss forming a community rugby club to develop players from the school who would normally be lost to rugby.

As well as these local people, adverts in the Oxford Mail and the Littlemore Local newsletter brought several more from the community and the meeting was duly held, well attended, in the school. His proposal was greeted with enthusiasm. A committee was formed with a President, Chairman, Secretary and Treasurer: Littlemore RFC was born!

In October, ex-pupils of the school, some staff from local banks, and wearing borrowed shirts (all white) from Oxon. Colts, Littlemore RFC took the field for an inaugural fixture against High Wycombe Bodgers. As expected they went down heavily to a more experienced side but went on to play over ten games in their first season.

In the second season they fielded a regular second XV and later on occasions, an experimental (and short lived) third XV – they even managed to field a Colts XV too.

The local influence of Lynn was attracting more players to this small community club which was making its name in Oxford and a highlight of those early years was reaching the semi-final of the Oxfordshire KO Cup when they defeated Oxford RFC, the most senior of several clubs in Oxford at that time. They also defeated Henley. Some 'senior' clubs were wrong-footed by the quality of Littlemore.RFC!

Lynn continued to coach the club, and even to turn out to play for them until the late 1980s, and was instrumental in obtaining permission from the school to convert a redundant teaching building into a clubhouse which was opened in 1985. It was believed to be the first licensed independent rugby club on school premises in the country. The clubhouse remains a community hub and hosts darts clubs, pigeon clubs and Aunt Sally clubs supported by local people. It is also the spiritual home of their local rugby club.

Around this time Lynn started a successful 15 years of coaching at Oxford University RFC, developing his 'game based' philosophy on coaching.

In 1997 Lynn was persuaded to leave coaching at Littlemore RFC and to join Chinnor RFC who were progressing through local leagues and needed the innovative and enlightened style of coaching which Lynn offered. He was instrumental in their promotion to National League status.

Back at Littlemore RFC and moving forward to 2019, the club had, following a stellar 3-year period, gained two consecutive promotions and reached Southern Counties North for the first time in their history. Then the club hit a wall and were relegated twice, losing players and facing the prospect of not even raising one XV team.

Step up the Welsh Wizard! Despite having celebrated his 80th birthday he was as sprightly as ever and was determined not to see the club he had founded disappear. On with the tracksuit and back to coaching the young (and old) in the white and royal blue of Littlemore RFC, doing what he loves best after 70 years of rugby.

Rob Egerton

OURFC, Sydney University and Australia

I first met Lynn after arriving in Oxford from Australia in 1987. Being a shy Australian, which apparently broke the perceived stereotype, I struggled with the formality of the Oxford way of life. Lynn immediately set me at ease with his relaxed approach and welcoming way. Before long I felt as if I was part of his extended family, regularly visiting his home in Littlemore and even looking after it during extended term breaks when I was in need of somewhere to stay. He had a knack of setting new arrivals at ease with his quirky ways and his "none too serious" approach. I appreciated, too, his acceptance of me as a player. In an era when fullbacks were renowned for their booming boots (think Roger Gould or Paul Thorburn), I was one who rarely kicked and thought of counter-attack as my first option. Lynn embraced this, was never critical, and built it into his attacking game-plans.

As a rugby coach he had a few memorable traits. Firstly, he was one of the early proponents of giving his players a voice. He would be the first to admit that in a team that included a World Cup winning All Black captain, as well as a multitude of current or former international players, there was both knowledge and experience that could be added to his input. The 1988 Oxford Blues team, which probably still ranks as one of the best ever, had a collection of strong personalities that all needed a say. I can remember many discussions with Lynn about why particular moves were played and on-field decisions were made. His management and gentle approach were key reasons for that team's success. So too was his rugby philosophy. He introduced us to the ideas of legendary French coach Pierre Villepreux, who he invited for a session at Iffley Road. His ideas of teaching awareness of space and support through modified games resonated with us and I believe was something that Lynn carried with him during his long coaching career. I certainly adopted it in my own coaching.

Off the field Lynn had a spirit of mischief which rubbed off on his team. His role as choirmaster meant that we were never short of a tune to repay the hospitality of our hosts. Whether responding to the tie-waving antics of Waseda University in Japan or simply on long bus trips on tour, the "coal" song and Lynn's medley bound the team and are still rattling around in my head 30 years later. He adopted and adapted from everywhere he went. On a 7's tour to Paris, we played pétanque between games and soon it became a staple wherever we were. On tour in Japan, Yatakas (bathrobes) were "donated" from each of the hotels we stayed. On returning to Oxford, Lynn held a novel birthday party at his home where the dress code was "Yutaka only" and the party game was petanque. Only Lynn could carry it off! Lynn is a great rugby man who has maintained his sense of fun throughout his long career. He continues to question and learn about the game. It would be impossible to count the number of players and coaches he has influenced. I am certainly one of them.

Mark Egan
OURFC Captain 1990

Having played rugby from the age of seven for close to twenty five years, I was fortunate to have been tutored in the game by many dedicated and competent coaches. They all had an individual style and philosophy that was unique to them and there is no question that Lynn was the most inspiring coach I had the pleasure of playing under. Lynn is first and foremost a teacher and brought enthusiasm and passion to his coaching style, which was entirely focused on team and individual development in an open and enjoyable learning and playing environment. Lynn truly believes in Rugby's character building values and his long and distinguished coaching career was underpinned by an unwavering commitment to living those values both on and off the field. At OURFC he is revered as much for his coaching success with various Blues teams as he is for his post-match renditions of "Coal from the Rhondda" and other memorable Welsh ditties!! OURFC was blessed to have had Lynn's services and those who were fortunate to have come under his tutelage on their rugby journey are without doubt better individuals because of him.

Dai Evans
OURFC, Cardiff and Wales

When I arrived in Oxford in '88, it was a very reassuring Welsh voice as head coach that welcomed us. Lynn was a very thoughtful, analytical coach and effective communicator and was successful in getting the best out of all his players. As an outside half I was in my element because we shared a belief that a rugby field was a place where you needed to express yourself and make the most of your natural talent. He was an inclusive coach and an exponent of attacking rugby, encouraging you to think about the game and to become an important part of the coaching strategy. This approach created an environment that allowed your confidence to thrive and it developed a very cohesive group of players. Lynn was one of very few coaches I worked with that effortlessly combined his extensive knowledge of the game with an infectious personality and character. He therefore gained your total respect as a coach and a person. I look back fondly at the time I spent at Oxford and the time I spent with Lynn. He is a very proud and passionate Welshman and after 30 years I am still honoured to call him my friend.

Andrew Williams
OURFC

Lynn, my fellow Welshman, always smiling, always welcoming, with a passion for playing exciting expansive rugby. That will always be my lasting impression of this great man. I was very fortunate to be part of the iconic 1988 side and privileged to have been coached by someone who was a visionary for the game. The way he shaped the '88 side from the September tour of Japan through to that emphatic victory against Cambridge in December was incredible – a professional approach during an amateur era, playing with style and playing with a smile. As a typical Welshman, Lynn did love to sing and he did have a knack of making bus journeys in Japan feel LONGER with his rendition of 'Dem Bones'! How many verses were in that song Lynn!! You are a legend in Oxford University rugby history, a legend in rugby and a legend of a man.

John Vaughan
Scrum half and captain Chinnor RFC 1996 - 2005

Lynn arrived at Chinnor as Head Coach in the pre-season of 1997/8 season. This was a major coup for the club as Lynn had a stellar reputation having coached Oxford University for 15 years in the heyday of Varsity Rugby, where he had coached many of the world's leading players. He was also one of the leading thinkers and philosophers of the game and his long standing and deep relationship with legendary Frenchmen Pierre Villepreux helped influence his vision. Ken Vaughan and Kevin Robinson led the pursuit for Lynn and eventually, luckily, he cracked. Lynn later admitted he got a bit fed up making up excuses to say no to Ken, and his leap of faith was made easier by the relationship between two passionate, rugby and wine loving Welshmen. This relationship flourished throughout Lynn's relationship with Chinnor and was fundamental to our success on and off the pitch.

Lynn had an immediate and transformative impact on the club, not just the 1st team but throughout the playing ranks, senior. junior and mini. His passion, humour and infectious personality coupled with his deep knowledge of the game was a heady mix and quickly won over many dyed in the wool exponents of 10-man rugby. With a focus on improving core skills and players finding space by introducing small sided games in training the impact was remarkable. He could persuade players to do things even they thought impossible and turned previously one -dimensional players into multi skilled exponents and thinkers of the game. It felt like an honour to be coached and spend time in his company.

In a way Lynn had a blank canvas to work on but he encountered a squad of players who were eager to learn and improve and more than willing to stretch themselves and take on new and innovative ideas. With the ball in operation during pre-season and an opportunity to compete against each other in training games the enjoyment and the skill improvements were immense. He would sometimes leave many a forward bewildered as he asked a player to charge at him and expertly time a deft pass to release a supporting player, or just softly lift an off-load into the space he has just vacated. The penny would drop and the skill level would raise another step.

The style of rugby was fast and free flowing and a joy to play with all players encouraged to handle and support the ball. It inevitably led to success on the pitch with promotions and cup victories, including an epic victory against Banbury at Oxford University ground, Iffley Road which was very poignant for Lynn. He often arranged coaching sessions at Oxford University if the weather was too bad to train outdoors, which also led to an increase in S&C as well as skills.

There were set-backs and these could lead to some forensic straight talking in the changing rooms and at training. After one heavy defeat at Dorchester Lynn administered a force 10 rollicking to the boys individually picking on who and what went wrong, with the players looking at the floor hoping they would not be the next in the spotlight. Ben Phillips, whose opposite number had scored a hat trick, was happily surprised that he had missed out on any vitriol as Lynn's summary seemingly had come to an end. Silence abounded the changing room as Lynn then turned to Ben and uttered the immortal words "And as for you Lord Lucan..." These were moments made all the more memorable for their rarity.

Not content with improving the boys as players Lynn also managed to gel the squad into a more than passable male voice choir. The long trips back from the west country flew past as Lynn honed the singing like a masterful maestro with renditions of, When the coal comes from the Rhondda, Dem Bones and Hymns and Arias. Although he was sometimes bemused by the amount of liquid consumed before the singing would begin. He was also a founder member of the Gourmet Club, a dedicated group of coaches, committee and supporters who would indulge themselves in fine wine and food as they dissected the game on the way home. In later years Lynn would entertain everyone at the Christmas party with a medley of his greatest hits including his 12 Days of Christmas Tour de Force.

Lynn's influence and playing philosophy throughout the club was established and still remains with Lynn running many 'coach the coaches' forums and happily helping out with his coaching masterclasses right across the age groups. His huge network of rugby contacts meant players were also privileged to be coached by the likes of French coaches Didier Retiere and Emile N'tamack, and specialist scrummaging sessions which dramatically improved an already strong set-piece. Lynn also arranged for groups of players to attend summer rugby camps in France. If Toulouse were using the same techniques and skills then we must have been doing something right! And this added to the lore. The reputation for advanced coaching and open rugby meant the club also attracted better players willing to learn and standards constantly improved. Not forgetting that Mary, Lynn's wife, was very generous in her allocation of Wimbledon tickets which could often lead to the rather incongruous sight of Cliff Richard sitting next to cauliflowered eared props on centre court.

A proud Welshman, a visionary rugby man, a true gentleman and philosopher of the game who it seems is happiest coaching on a wet and windy night, a great Chinnor clubman. We are very proud to have Lynn as an Honorary Life Member. We only hope Lynn enjoyed his time with us half as much as we did, his influence on and off the pitch live on with many ex- players using his ideas and methods coaching mini and juniors.

Magnus Eyles

Deputy Head, Kingham Hill School

Kingham Hill School has had a long tradition of supporting pupils from under-priviliged backgrounds, many of whom come with social needs. The rugby programme at the school has played an intrinsic part in the personal development of many of our pupils but its positive impact has been most often marked in those pupils from difficult home lives. Effective rugby teams are a brotherhood or a sisterhood. There is a sense of belonging and acceptance which anyone who commits to such teams will benefit from. This is a critical foundation which many young people sadly lack. Cultures are powerful, so the characteristics they encourage and instil are important. Anyone who has played rugby will appreciate that the culture encourages loyalty, grit and discipline, which are vital characteristics in the wider world. Under Lynn Evans, we have built upon other treasured benefits of the rugby mentality. The need for honest appraisal.

Many pupils have developed the ability to be objective about how to overcome barriers to progress and development. It is difficult to put into words just how helpful this skill has been when transferred into conversations about real life issues in the lives of some of the young people who have come through the school. For some pupils, these have been emotive issues which they have never been able to engage with before. While many of these things would be true in lots of rugby clubs and schools across the country, the style of coaching which Lynn Evans has brought to the school has had an impact which I have not seen anywhere else before.

The game based approach to coaching has drawn players into the programme for the sheer love and enjoyment of playing. Games teachers everywhere will appreciate the effort required to persuade anxious newcomers to play rugby at all. Striving to keep the ball alive and avoiding contact, if possible, has encouraged more timid pupils to grow in confidence and it's fair to say some of our best players were very nervous about rugby at the outset. Pupils thoroughly enjoy this style of learning and playing the game. Again, we have seen the pastoral benefits of this beyond the school's playing fields. The other key aspect from which we have benefitted is the player-centred approach of Lynn's coaching. Training individuals to think and make decisions for themselves has had a radical impact on our pupils both on and off the field.

As playbooks gave way to principles we have enjoyed a much richer, diverse and exciting form of rugby at Kingham Hill. Young people seem almost afraid to make their own decisions in the current youth culture. As such, the benefits of coaching a style which demands they do this has been hugely beneficial for them and set foundations which will put these pupils in good stead for later life. Staff and pupils are indebted to the rugby culture, which Lynn has developed at the school.

Mike Tanner

Oxfordshire Schools 19 Group 1963-64; 1964-65
Oxfordshire Schools 19 Group 1963-64; 1964-65
Oxfordshire 1965-66; 1972-73
Oxford University 1966-67; 1967-68; 1968-69
Leicestershire 1972-73
Hon Coach Leicester Tigers Youth 1977-78

I was a lazy 14-year-old footballer when Lynn Evans arrived at Littlemore Grammar School in 1961.Lynn proceeded to shape my destiny. Within four years he manufactured a scrum-half equipped to represent Oxfordshire in the County Championship, then not far off the highest level of the English senior game. And though others inspired me to apply to Oxford University it was Lynn who gave me the tools to win a place at the University's premier rugby college, St Edmund Hall.

171

Lynn came to a school open for three years that housed barely 170 pupils, half of them girls. We had a soccer team but a Welshman has other ideas: rugby was on the agenda. Lynn lined us up along the touchline and asked our names. On hearing mine he exclaimed: 'Hadyn Tanner! Best scrum-half of all time! With that name you can be my scrum-half.'

Somehow Lynn conjured up a XV from the 40-odd older boys for LGS to play its first organised game of rugby in the spring of 1962 against Burford GS - and we won. Though victories were rare for this small pool of inexperienced players, Lynn ensured anyone showing promise played for Oxford RFC Colts. Many a Saturday saw me turn out for School in the morning and Colts in the afternoon; and Charlie Ede's 'legendary' Oxford Thursday XV beckoned once physical maturity allowed.

From the outset Lynn 'coached' - unheard of in the '60s. No meagre diet of lapping, sprinting and physical jerks. Much was one-on-one. He'd take me out during the lunch hour to practise kicking, once ordering me to remove a spanking new pair of Elmer Cotton boots so that I might 'feel the ball, caress it and persuade it where to go and what to do.' I thought he'd lost his marbles; but Lynn taught me the rugby ball has its 'sweet spot.'

Lynn's impact at LGS and its successor Peers School (famed for its seven-a-side prowess) is epitomised by the series of quality players his talents produced: Ian Ray represented England Schools 15 Group; while Alan Jenkins (A rugby Blue at Oxford) Seretse Williams and Roy Davies, for example, were others from the second generation who won senior representative honours.

It's with immense pleasure, and no less pride, that I recall making my senior debut at Oxford RFC with Lynn as my half-back partner; and he was a team-mate proffering advice and encouragement in Oxfordshire colours. It came as no surprise to see him become a respected coach throughout the world; he praises his selfless service to the game he's loved all his life and to which he's dedicated his life are many and fully merit

Gary Henderson

Head of RFU Community Coaching

I was fortunate to meet Lynn in 1996 when we were both Youth Development Officers, (YDOs). Listening then to his passion for rugby and how the game should be coached and played made a significant impact upon me then as a player and as a coach. When I was appointed RFU Head of Coach & Player Development we were fortunate to call upon Lynn's expertise to help transform the way we developed the nation's coaches and players. Together with Pierre Villpreux, Lynn helped refine our development programmes to encourage coaches to become less drill-based and rigid in their coaching and establish a game-centred approach that encouraged players to solve problems and make better decisions. Even as he approached retirement, Lynn was still fascinated in developing his and others coaching craft. Whether this was running coaching experiments at schools, or when we travelled to France, South Africa, Malta, Malaysia, Canada and USA preaching the gospel to a new range of coaches, Lynn's appetite for rugby was only matched by his appetite for red wine and leading the singing.

Craig Brown,
CEO Penguin Rugby

Robbo called me and said I have this great Welshman who would be ideal for the work the Penguins are doing with coach development. OK I said, great, send me his details. A few months later Lynn made his first Penguin journey to Kuala Lumpur in April 2006 in the company of Penguin coaches.

Craig Brown and Mal Chumley to run a Level one coach's course. We met at the airport and the rest is history as they say.

What was striking about Lynn was his beaming smile, passion for the game, knowledge bank, ability to transfer this knowledge and the canny knack he has in story-telling. Many an evening was spent discussing his wide array of memories on the game and also his views on the development of coaches and in particular how you introduce rugby to children. It was certainly a player centric focus and Lynn was adamant there should be no scrums or lineouts in the first few years. Just running, handling, find space, scoring tries and much enjoyment.

Lynn travelled to Europe, Africa and Asia with the Penguins and always made a huge impact when coaching and of course made new friends all the time. It is always a pleasure to travel with Lynn.

APPENDIX 1
INSPIRING COMMENTS
FROM SOME SPECIAL COACHES

Iain McGeehan
British Lions Coach
'I try to think how the player is seeing the situation on the field and not what the detached view the coach is observing.'

Ben Ryan
Fiji Sevens Coach
'Now Sevens is an Olympic sport it means for some countries Sevens goes into the school curriculum and suddenly the game has many more players playing the game. El Salvador has started up a Sevens programme, it is played in all the schools in Russia, and Poland had ten new Sevens clubs in just a year.'

Rob Egerton
Oxford University and Australia player and former Australian team manager
'Ball in play in Fifteens is increasing and I wonder if some of that has come from the Sevens game. I think there is a butterfly flapping its wings somewhere that might have made the difference!

With risk taking there are inevitably some mistakes, but as coaches ourselves we know that, but cannot expect these players to open up defences if their attacking options become limited.

When we play as kids, we practice ball games and trying tricks. That's why you get guys like Quade Cooper, James O'Connor and Kurtley Beale, who are risk takers; they have always had it in their blood. They enjoy being inventive. Their first option is to have a crack.'

Wayne Smith
New Zealand coach
'I think it is the game of today because as coach I work on the fundamental principles of rugby of going forward and how to support, where to support, why to penetrate and why to play wide. These decisions are the decisions of the player, not the decision of the coach and I try to coach that. I try to give the player the liberty and possibility to take the initiative where the other players can see he plays like that.

When I coached the Crusaders, I put into practice my belief that players should be involved in the coaching process. Too often coaches took the responsibility away from the players. Players have to make decisions on the field, so they must practice these in the coaching environment. The problem is players want to be told because it is easier.

As a young coach it was hard. I did not believe in the 'motivating coach', but the hard-working coach who leads by example. The players were asked to take more responsibility. They were not used to it.

Most if not all the players were coming from coaching environments where they were not asked to take much responsibility.

Players teach each other when they are engaged in the process of player centred coaching. E.g., what we did when I was at Northampton RFC. We did it with New Zealand, a 20-minute session with one-on-one coaching by the players, making use of the experience in the squad, (New players need some help). The players design the drills and consult the coaches if they need some help. They are coaching themselves. Why teach stealing the ball in a tackle when we have Ritchie McCaw there.

My first coaching experience as a player/coach was in Italy. I liked what the other coaches and players were doing; their style of coaching as they talked a lot about movement of the players in the game. The skills could develop based on the necessity for the game. Also, I was in a very different culture than I was used to. I knew what the players wanted and tried to give it to them. It inspired me to go into coaching full time.

Sometimes you have to tell players what you want but I move along the line of delivery in coaching spending less time on tell and spend most of the time letting players make decisions for themselves.

When I first started using questioning with players during coaching sessions the questions were often too judgemental and leading. I needed to be more effective with my questions. I practised at home with my family! It is no good just asking 'Why did you do that?' The question could describe some action, or a decision made, so the player has a clear picture of what you saw. The questions should be non-confrontational, non-judgemental, allowing the players freedom to describe their actions.

The high-performance department in New Zealand rugby are our greatest supporters in developing player-centred coaching. All age group teams are coached with the similar principles. Players are also allowed to make mistakes from which they can learn and are encouraged to try things. We are concerned that leadership skills are developed and involve a lot of sports psychology.

With leadership it is sharing their feelings, their views, how to develop leaders, decision makers, through self-correcting, and taking responsibility for their actions.

We will not sack them if they don't win, but we want to develop the qualities mentioned above.'

Rob Smith
Former London Wasps Academy Manager

'Also, the club embraces young players and the top coaches give them time – an important commodity. The club is also as inclusive as possible – respect, honesty and togetherness are an important part of the Wasps development programme!

The effect of the peer group within Wasps is very strong. The Academy players are not on the periphery in the coaching environment, they are involved with the senior players, and therefore the coaching ethos of the club. They experience the ups and downs of professional rugby. The experienced players help them to that next level.'

John Brierley
Former England Athletics Manager Commonwealth Games

'More understanding of how coaches can make best use of the plethora of highly useful psychological research, which has been produced over the last 20 years, is another area of continued development for higher performing athlete support. In England we have some fantastic coaches in athletics, as well as many other sports, and their passion, experiences and knowledge are starting to be passed down by fledgling mentorship programmes. Whilst they often have an effective working knowledge of the psychology of coaching this could be augmented by contemporary research from other systems to inform and enhance their working relationships with athletes.'

Kevin Bowring
Wales Coach and Elite Coach Manager RFU

'As regards the role of the coach, I would say firstly it is a game for the players, everything starts with the players and the coach is the sixteenth player. He is just part of the team. He should be an independent thinker and self-responsible. He should help prepare the player to deal with anything the opposition put to him.

We need to help the coach in his early development to challenge players through the use of questioning. We also need to ask the question: is your coaching structure hierarchical? For example, the head buffalo leads the herd, while the swans work as part of a team while in flight. The coach acts as a leader, helping serving players but not directing. The coach may give the direction with the players taking up the mantle and being part of the process.

The coach needs vision – clarity of the game being played. They need to look at other coaches and become a patchwork of those other coaches, eventually evolving a philosophy of their own. Even at National level, coaches need to evolve. I would say that moving from being an elite player to coach can take up to five years.

The role of the coach can be expressed in two elements, those being: how to coach, i.e., how competent are you in delivering? And what to coach; what tactical and technical knowledge do you have?

Elite players are normally fairly well versed with the 'what skills', but do not have much experience with the how to coach. This 'how to coach' would certainly apply to all levels of coaching.

Many professional players on the RFU Coaching Award show enormous potential but struggle with the concept of empowering players, trying to get them to be self-managing and self-reliant. Visionary players could see tactical options on the field; the problem for them is to help other players to see them. The challenge for them after qualification at Level 2 is how to become better coaches.

Values and principles are perhaps not as well developed in the new 'professional coach' as with former coaches with an educational background. These new professional coaches are embracing the 'process skills' so there is hope we can maintain the balance e.g., controlling the emotions during/immediately after matches.

To develop 'game sense' practices should be relevant to what the players understand in the game. At the top end of the game the coaches tend to control the content more. Coaches should understand how to structure the practice; how skill is learnt and used in the game. Looking at deliberate practice is not fun – you have to be obsessive. At the lower end of the game, it is more important to have fun. The 'safety first' concept is still strong in the philosophy of coaches. Perhaps the coach needs to know the player well and read what he does. Near the game practices develop this understanding.'

Chalky White
Legendary Leicester and RFU Coach
'Three vital ingredients for an effective coach; in your work pay attention to accuracy, precision and detail, so the player may reap the benefits of individual improvement.

Please do not use 'give away' words such as 'Stand deeper'. What does it mean, two metres, two chains, six fathoms? Be specific, for example, start off at two arms lengths or stand 2 metres back on the inside shoulder of the ball carrier.

Does your team have a playing strategy? Please do not tell me we have a game plan!'

'Does your number 7 really know what his role is within the team?'

Pierre Villepreux
French coach

'Don't spend time beating on a wall, hoping to transform it into a door.'

'The players have a problem with the go forward. The coaches are giving too much emphasis to the game on the lateral axis.'

He quietly moves into the coaching session and changes the emphasis of the practice to work on the long axis and the penetration game. Quite soon the penetration opportunities become evident. This is a knowledgeable mind at work!

Printed in Great Britain
by Amazon

75411500R00108